salvation is forever

salvation is forever

by
Robert Glenn Gromacki

❧ ❧ ❧
❧ ❧ ❧

MOODY PRESS
CHICAGO

Library of Congress Catalog Card Number: 73-7331

ISBN: 0-8024-7506-X

Second Printing, 1974

Printed in the United States of America

To
my parents

Contents

CHAPTER   PAGE

Preface   9

1. What Does It Mean to Be Lost?   13

2. What Does It Mean to Be Saved?   33

3. Does God Guarantee Our Salvation?   71

4. Do You Know These Scriptural Principles?   87

5. What About Those Problem Passages?   113

6. What Is Your Spiritual Condition?   170

Scripture Index   185

Preface

CAN A SAVED PERSON ever be lost? Can a Christian, a person who has received Jesus Christ as his personal Saviour, sin to such a degree that he will lose his salvation, go to hell or hades at death, and eventually be consigned to the lake of fire at the great white throne judgment? This question has also been worded in many other ways, familiar to most keen Bible students: Is a person once saved always saved? Is the expression, "Once in grace, always in grace" true? Do you believe in eternal security? Are you an Arminian or a Calvinist?

How many times have you heard those questions? Why bring them up now? Some feel that, since no one has settled this issue in the past, why try to solve it in the present? The attitude of many is "Let sleeping dogs (ie., doctrines) lie!" Nothing can be solved by resurrecting this sensitive area. Others add that the discussion of eternal security is divisive and not constructive.

Are these attitudes valid? Is there no place for a clear exposition of the biblical doctrine of eternal security? Is it a nonessential teaching, especially when the spirit of the age is clothed with ecumenical cooperation, even among Evangelicals? It is acceptable today to put away doctrinal differences in order to have a common testimony toward unbelievers and to have greater love and union among Christians. But, is it *right* to do so? All Bible doctrines are important and must be taught clearly in love. Man-made teachings can and should be discarded. This, then, is the problem. Is the doctrine of eternal security a clear scriptural teaching, or is it a fabrication of men's minds?

Where can a person get information on this problem? If you would go into a Bible bookstore, you would probably search in vain for a book exclusively devoted to this subject. To be sure, there are a few pamphlets and booklets in print on the topic, but they simply scan the question and the possible solution. Several theology textbooks have units on eternal security, but you would have to buy the entire book to get the value of a few pages. When it comes right down to it, there is little in print on the subject. There has been a lot of talking and arguing but little writing. One purpose of this book is to devote an entire volume to this very important subject, a book that can be put into the hands of interested inquirers. Regardless of what some church leaders say, the issue of the eternal security of a believer (pro or con) is still discussed fervently by the lay members of our churches, by students in colleges and in Bible institutes, and by most ministers who have to answer the questions of their congregations.

There is even a paradox in our churches. Some in Calvinistic churches wonder about the possible loss of their salvation. Some in Arminian churches are convinced of their own security.

The plan of this book will be to present the Scriptures pertinent to the subject and to expound those same biblical passages in the light of sound hermeneutical principles. I recognize that God is one and that His revelation is harmonious with His character. It is absolutely impossible to find within the Bible fifty passages that teach eternal security and fifty others that deny it. The Bible teaches *one* doctrine, not two contradictory positions. Only one can be correct. I believe that the true scriptural position is that a person who has been born into God's family through faith in Jesus Christ has *eternal* salvation. This means that there can be no loss of that salvation whatsoever. I admit that there are difficult passages, but these must be interpreted in the light of clear, self-evident passages of Scripture. This fact must be reiterated for emphasis: the Bible does not teach two opposite doctrines. This book will present basically a positive demonstration of the truth of eternal security. It will also deal with those passages that are used to attack this position.

If this book should be read by an unbeliever, I trust that the reader will see his lost, condemned position before God and receive God's gracious provision of eternal salvation through His Son, Jesus Christ. I also trust that this book will cause Christians to enjoy the salvation and peace provided by Christ. Too many have never experienced the joy of their salvation because they have lived with the fear that they could lose it. To serve God out of gratitude for what He has done is much better than to serve him out of anxiety.

1

What Does It Mean to Be Lost?

JESUS SAID that He came into the world to seek and to save those who are lost (Lk 19:10). He spoke about the *lost* sheep, the *lost* coin, and the *lost* son. The apostle Paul wrote that the gospel was hidden to those who are lost (2 Co 4:3). Why was the term *lost* used? What does it mean to be lost?

This is one of the biblical terms used to describe man's position or standing before God prior to personal salvation. It is God's assessment of the natural man. It implies that man is in a desperate condition and that he can do nothing to rescue himself from his dilemma. The unsaved man is unaware of his spiritual lostness until he is convicted of his moral plight by the Holy Spirit. However, the unusual paradox is the fact that many Christians themselves do not understand the lost condition from which they have been saved.

This first chapter will introduce the reader to the biblical reasons why a person who is not a Christian stands condemned before God as a guilty, lost sinner. When one understands fully what it means to be lost, then he will comprehend more thoughtfully and thankfully the scope of his salvation provided in Christ. Then, he can move on to a consideration of the next questions: Can a Christian lose his salvation? Can he again be lost and guilty before

God? Because, if a person can lose his salvation, he must return *exactly* and *completely* to that position which he once had before God; not just to a *partial* lost condition, but to a *total* lost postion. So, now we shall consider the question, Why are people guilty and lost before God?

First, their rejection of divine revelation condemns them. Divine revelation is truth that God has revealed or communicated to men. The author of Hebrews wrote, "God, who at sundry times and in divers manners spake in time past unto the fathers by the prophets, Hath in these last days spoken unto us by his Son" (Heb 1:1-2a). Ever since creation, God has revealed truth about Himself and His will at different times in various ways. Truth is not just to be learned but also to be done. God holds men accountable for what He has given to them, and all men of all ages have received some form of divine revelation.

God has revealed Himself through nature or creation. David sang, "The heavens declare the glory of God; and the firmament showeth his handywork" (Ps 19:1). He later wrote, "I will praise thee; for I am fearfully and wonderfully made" (Ps 139:14). The stars, the planets, the sky, the hills and mountains, the rivers and oceans, and our very physical bodies, were designed to reveal truth about God's character and being. Only the fool would deny the existence of God as he studies the world through the telescope or the microscope (Ps 14:1). Paul stated that God's existence, His power, and His intelligence, can be known by every man through nature (Ro 1:19-20). However, because of their sinful bias, men "hold the truth in unrighteousness" (Ro 1:18). Although the intricacies of inner and outer space argue for the existence of an intelligent designer, a moral personality, some men refuse to admit this. They would rather believe that the world just evolved by impersonal forces from embryonic beginnings in a primeval chemical sea. To admit the existence of a God who created them would imply moral responsibility to that God, and this they refuse to do. They suppress the truth because they do not want to change their behavior. They justify their decision, however, in the guise of intellectual honesty and scientific observation. This man—the college graduate, the PhD, the scientist—is "without excuse" before God (Ro 1:20) because he has rejected what God has designed to be perceived by the human mind.

The heathen in the backward countries are in the same moral dilemma as the sophisticated American intellectual. He does not deny the existence of deity when he looks at nature; he multiplies his gods. He changes "the glory of the uncorruptible God into an image made like to corruptible man, and to birds, and fourfooted beasts, and creeping things" (Ro 1:23). He does not deny God; he just doesn't worship Him! He worships the creation rather than the Creator. He distorts truth. He falls down before a piece of wood, the sun, a dumb animal, and sometimes even before a fellow human being who is just as sinful as he is. For this action, God holds the heathen accountable. Because they live from the cradle to the grave without acknowledging the true God of nature, they stand condemned and will spend eternity separated from God. Man has played the fool by denying or perverting the truth of God revealed in nature.

God has also revealed truth about Himself through man's personality. God created man in His own image (Gen 1:26-27); therefore, the image of God in man must reflect some truth about the nature and character of God. This image is still retained by man, even after the fall of Adam and the entrance of sin into the world (Gen 9:6). What is this image? It cannot refer to man's physical body, because God is a spirit being (Jn 4:24). It must refer to man's immaterial being—to his soul or spirit—to the fact that he is a moral personality. Like God, he has intellect, emotion, and will. Also, like God and unlike the animal creation, he has a sense of moral oughtness, a conscience, an indicator of right and wrong.

As man looks into his inner self, either casually or through a psychological study, he is aware that he is a moral being and that he is a created being. Where does this awareness come from? Where did the idea of good and evil originate? Man *should* come to the conclusion that a moral God has created him and that he is morally responsible to this God for his wrong attitudes and actions. He *should* fall down before this holy God and ask for forgiveness for his sin, but he does not. Why? Because he rejects his moral responsibility for his deeds. He either puts the blame on someone else or else justifies his actions (Ro 2:15). Adam blamed Eve, and Eve blamed the serpent. Pity the serpent! It had no one to blame except God, and that is exactly what some people do today. They blame God for their sin. Some excuse their sin by saying they are not as bad as others. Today, some new moralists justify immorality outside of the marriage bond by claiming that there is sometimes more love outside of marriage than within marriage. Do two wrongs make a right? Never. Man rejects the truth of God's holy personality when he finds excuses for his unrighteousness. For this action, God holds him accountable (Ro 2:1).

So far, we have looked at the divine truth revealed to the uncivilized heathen and to the civilized pagan. To natural revelation (creation and man's personality) God has added specific data in the form of special revelation. This special revelation is the Bible, God's written word. All scripture is the inspired, or the "breathed out" Word of God (2 Ti

3:16). It is what God would *say* directly to man if He were using this method of revelation today. The Bible did not originate within the thought processes of men, but God directed men by the Holy Spirit to write what He wanted to communicate in human language, words capable of being understood by man (2 Pe 1:20-21).

This was the advantage that the Jewish nation enjoyed. To them were committed the oracles of God (Ro 3:2). God gave His moral commandments in written form (Ex 20), His law through Moses—Genesis to Deuteronomy—and His Word through Jewish prophets after the pattern of Moses (Deu 18:15-22). Moses wrote, "The secret things belong unto the LORD our God: but those things which are revealed belong unto us and to our children for ever, that we may do all the words of this law" (Deu 29:29). Israel knew more about God and His revealed will than the ungodly Gentile nations that surrounded her, *but* she rejected this extra truth. She broke the law of God at its very inception; she refused to repent under the preaching ministry of the prophets; and in conclusion, she rejected the very Messiah toward whom the Old Testament pointed (Lk 24:44; Jn 5:46). The biblical principle is that to "whomsoever much is given, of him shall be much required" (Lk 12:48). God gave more truth to Israel; therefore, Israel was more accountable to God. This is why Jesus said it would be *more* tolerable for Sodom and Tyre in the day of judgment than for the Jewish cities to which He ministered (Mt 11:20-24). The Old Testament cities had rejected the messages of holy men, but the cities of Judea and of Galilee had rejected the very person of God Himself.

Today, most men within Christendom and even throughout the world fall under the same indictment as ancient Israel. The New Testament, containing the significance of

Christ's person and redemptive work, combined with the
Old Testament, gives to man God's total revelation of Himself and His program for the ages. The Bible is available
practically everywhere. It is there to be read, to be understood, and to be believed. But what does modern man do?
He regards it as just another piece of ancient literature,
containing primitive religious concepts. He feels that it is
not worth his time to investigate its teachings. When he
does read, he rejects what he finds—the revelation of his
sinful character and of God's holy being. He does not receive "the things of the Spirit of God: for they are foolishness unto him" (1 Co 2:14). God holds men responsible
for their rejection of His Word.

For men to be saved, they must receive by faith the
Christ of the gospel message—the one who died for their
sins according to the scriptures, was buried, and who rose
again according to the scriptures (1 Co 15:1-4). When a
person comes under the hearing of the gospel message, he
then becomes accountable for his moral response. He can
either accept or reject, but he cannot remain neutral. If
he rejects, God holds him guilty. If he regards the message
of the cross as foolishness, then he is numbered among
those who are perishing (1 Co 1:18). "He that believeth
on him is not condemned: but he that believeth not is
condemned already, because he hath not believed in the
name of the only begotten Son of God" (Jn 3:18). Rejection of the gospel and of Christ brings additional condemnation to the unsaved man.

All men are guilty before God because they have rejected divine revelation, no matter what form it has taken—
creation, the image of God in man, the Bible, or the written
and oral message of the cross.

There is a second basic reason why men are lost and
guilty. Their relationship to the world condemns them.

All unsaved people are citizens of this world. As "world patriots," they love this world system and are opposed to all who are not part of it. A Christian has been chosen out of the world by Christ (Jn 15:19). He has also been given out of the world by the Father to the Son (Jn 17:6). True to his loyalty, the worldling hates and persecutes the Christian because the system to which he belongs hated and persecuted Christ 1900 years ago (Jn 15:18-19). The world loves its own, but a Christian is no longer a member of the world family. Jesus said that His kingdom was not of this world (Jn 18:36). This world is unalterably opposed to Christ's kingdom, the "other world," of which each Christian is a citizen. This is not an East-West conflict but a heaven-earth opposition. God loves, but the world hates.

The unsaved man is also a world conformist. He walks "according to the course of this world" (Eph 2:2). His pleasures are world-centered; his values are world-oriented; his ambitions are world-directed. He is not God-centered or directed. He is dominated by the philosophy of this age. His dress, his diet, and his desires all reflect the bias and prejudice of his world conformity. He has no desire to bring God into the center of his experience. A friend of the world is naturally the enemy of God (Ja 4:4). As long as a person remains a world citizen and conformer, he is lost.

Third, their relationship to Satan condemns them. Contrary to popular opinion, Satan is a real, personal being, not a Halloween-fabricated character. He was a created cherub (Eze 28:12-19) who sinned against God. His wisdom and beauty led to pride and his subsequent downfall (Is 14:12-17). Since his fall, he has become the archenemy of God and of His program. One day, he will be cast into the lake of fire, where he will be tormented forever and ever (Mt 25:41; Rev 20:10). In his opposition to God,

Satan sustains a definite relationship to the world of mankind. Through his temptation, Eve ate of his forbidden fruit in the garden of Eden (Gen 3). He has been active in the world of human affairs ever since. How has man been affected by this sinful being?

Every sinner is actually a "spiritual" child of the devil. He manifests this by not doing righteousness and by not loving Christians (1 Jn 3:10). Spiritual children of God are just the opposite in position and in practice. They do righteousness and they love their brothers in Christ. Jesus told His Jewish opponents that if God had been their Father, they would have loved Him because He came from God (Jn 8:42). He added:

> Why do ye not understand my speech? even because ye cannot hear my word.
>
> Ye are of your father the devil, and the lusts of your father ye will do. He was a murderer from the beginning, and abode not in the truth, because there is no truth in him. When he speaketh a lie, he speaketh of his own: for he is a liar, and the father of it (Jn 8:43-44).

Like begets like. All unsaved people do not love Christ with their total being because Satan, their father, does not love Him. They do not respond to the divine word, they hate or murder, they lie—all because of their spiritual, satanic nature. Just as Satan stands condemned for his character and actions, so his children are condemned.

Not only is Satan a father to sinners, but Paul calls him a ruler. Read Paul's description of his conversion experience: "Who [Christ] hath delivered us from the power of darkness, and hath translated us into the kingdom of his dear Son" (Col 1:13). Christians are now in Christ's spiritual kingdom; they were once under Satan's rule. The extent of satanic dominion is little known today, yet Jesus called him "the prince of this world" (Jn 12:31). Paul called him "the prince of the power of the air" (Eph 2:2) and "the god of this world" (2 Co 4:4). The Christian daily wrestles "against principalities, against powers, against the rulers of the darkness of this world, against spiritual wickedness in high places" (Eph 6:12). When Satan offered Christ the kingdoms of this world, Jesus did not doubt his ability to give them (Mt 4:8-9). These passages clearly show that Satan rules over a world of fallen angels and sinful men. They are in his kingdom. They not only obey him, they worship him.

The unsaved person is also under the direct control of the devil. According to Paul, he walks not only in conformity to the world but also "according to the prince of the power of the air" (Eph 2:2). He is a "Satan-conformist!" He walks according to satanic goals, likes, and dislikes. Paul adds the thought that the devil is a "spirit that now worketh in the children of disobedience" (Eph 2:2). The Greek idea behind "worketh" is energy. Satan energizes the unsaved. He works in and through them to accomplish his will. From this passage, it is easy to see that no unsaved man has a totally free will. An anti-Christ will is steering the car of his life.

Just as a child sits in the lap of his father, "the whole world lieth in wickedness" (1 Jn 5:19). The phrase "in wickedness" can better be translated "in the wicked one." The world is in the lap of the wicked one, or the devil. The impression conveyed is that the devil is in control of the world system and that the world cannot do anything about its predicament.

Finally, Satan blinds the minds and spiritual perception of lost people. Paul said that "the god of this world hath blinded the minds of them which believe not, lest the light of the glorious gospel of Christ, who is the image of God, should shine unto them" (2 Co 4:4). When man's physical

eyes are blinded, he cannot see the natural light of the *sun;*
when man's mind or spiritual eyes are blinded, he cannot
see the spiritual light of the *Son.* Jesus is the light of men.
He shines in a world of spiritual darkness, but blinded men
do not receive Him (Jn 1:4-5). Most men do not believe
that they are spiritually blind. That is exactly what Satan
wants them to believe. That is part of his plan of deception. This is what Jesus meant in His evaluation of the
Pharisees: "If ye were blind, ye should have no sin: but
now ye say, We see; therefore your sin remaineth" (Jn
9:41). When men think that they can understand spiritual
truth but they really cannot, then Satan has succeeded in
blinding them. When men admit their spiritual blindness,
then they have taken the first step. Paul said that unsaved
Gentiles walk "in the vanity of their mind, having the understanding darkened, being alienated from the life of God
through the ignorance that is in them, because of the blindness of their heart" (Eph 4:17-18). Satan's goal is to keep
sinners from the life of God. He does this by dulling their
spiritual perception. Have you ever wondered why so
many PhDs reject the simple truth of Scripture? For the
same reason the illiterate reject it: Satan has cast a cloud
over their hearts. Just as God created light to dispel the
darkness (Gen 1:3), so God today must create spiritual
light to dispel man's moral blindness (2 Co 4:6).

Fourth, man is condemned because of his relationship
to sin. *Sin!* A forgotten word in the vocabulary of modern
man. He has invented different terms to take its place:
mistakes, hangups, ills, et cetera. But God calls it sin. Sin
is any lack of conformity to the character and will of God.
In many ways, man has come short of God's holy standard.

The Bible declares that man sinned in Adam. Paul
wrote, "Wherefore, as by one man sin entered into the
world, and death by sin; and so death passed upon all men,

for that all have sinned" (Ro 5:12). We know that all men die physically, but when did all men sin? When did the infant who dies sin? This is a hard theological question, but there is a scriptural answer. When Adam sinned, every man (potentially present in the genetic makeup of Adam) sinned. When Adam sinned, you sinned in him. When Adam sinned, I sinned in him. God reckons Adam's sin to be your sin and my sin.

An illustration is in order here. The book of Hebrews argues that the priesthood of Melchisedec is greater than that of Levi. To prove it, the author refers to the time when Abraham, the great-grandfather of Levi, paid tithes to Melchisedec. Here is the conclusion of the argument: "And as I may so say, Levi also, who receiveth tithes, payed tithes in Abraham, For he was yet in the loins of his father, when Melchisedec met him" (Heb 7:9-10). Levi, yet unborn, paid tithes in Abraham. So we, yet unborn, sinned in Adam. We participated personally, yet unconsciously, in Adam's sin. If we had been in that garden instead of Adam, we would have done the very same thing that Adam and Eve did. We are just like Adam, bone of his bone and flesh of his flesh.

God declared the penalty of sin even before Adam disobeyed the divine will: "But of the tree of the knowledge of good and evil, thou shalt not eat of it: for in the day that thou eatest thereof thou shalt surely die" (Gen 2:17). When Adam sinned, he died spiritually and he began to die physically. The processes of corruption and mortality set into his body. His state of spiritual death became immediately evident by his shame for his nakedness, by his hiding from God, and by his excusing of his sin (Gen 3:7-13). Every man born into the world not only participates in Adam's sin but also in his punishment. He is born dead in sins, and the body of the infant is destined to disease and to death.

Adam became guilty before God because of his sin of rebellion; so we are guilty before God because we were in Adam. Consider these verses carefully:

> For if through the offence of one many be dead . . . for the judgment was by one to condemnation . . .
> For if by one man's offence death reigned by one . . . Therefore as by the offence of one judgment came upon all men to condemnation . . . For as by one man's disobedience many were made sinners . . . (Ro 5:15-19).

This is a difficult truth but a scriptural one. One reason why men are lost is that they have sinned in Adam.

Men are also guilty because they have inherited a sin nature from their ancestral father, Adam. The principle "after its kind" is indelibly written into God's created world. Birds beget birds, dogs beget dogs, cats beget cats, and sinful men beget sinful men. No children were born to Adam and Eve before their disobedience, but after the fall, the famous brothers Cain and Abel were born. Were they born with a sin nature? Did they have an inbred propensity to rebel? Cain was jealous and angry at Abel and finally killed him. Proof enough! Adam's sons were begotten in his likeness and image (Gen 5:3). They were no different than he was—no worse, no better—in their position before God. Adam sinned; so they sinned. Adam died; so they died.

The presence of the sin nature has thoroughly corrupted man's total being. His personality—intellect, emotion, and will—is turned away from God and toward sin. His understanding is "darkened, being alienated from the life of God through the ignorance that is in them, because of the blindness of their heart" (Eph 4:18). His heart "is deceitful above all things, and desperately wicked" (Jer 17:9).

His will is enslaved to sin, uncleanness, and iniquity (Ro 6:17-19).

David was aware of man's inherited sinfulness when he wrote: "Behold, I was shapen in iniquity; and in sin did my mother conceive me" (Ps 51:5). Unaware of contemporary, sophisticated, genetic knowledge, David nevertheless traced his sin problem to his fetal state. He was born in sin. God gave this evaluation of man after the flood: "For the imagination of man's heart is evil from his youth" (Gen 8:21). Man does not have to be taught to sin; he knows how intuitively.

Men are also guilty because of their sinful acts and attitudes. These acts and attitudes are the natural expression or fruit of the sin nature. An apple tree is an apple tree long before it produces apples because it has the nature of an apple tree. So it is with man. He is a sinner in nature long before he puts forth the blooms of his sinful attitudes and the fruit of his sinful deeds. But just as the apple tree manifests its nature, so the sinner will manifest his. He does it in two ways: by his thoughts and emotions and by his willful decisions.

All men have broken the moral law of God in these two areas. No one has kept it in his heart or done it with his hand. The sinful act is the manifestation of the sinful attitude. God holds man responsible for both. Jesus said,

> "That which cometh out of the man, that defileth the man. For from within, out of the heart, proceed evil thoughts, adulteries, fornications, murders, thefts, covetousness, wickedness, deceit, lasciviousness, an evil eye, blasphemy, pride, foolishness: All these evil things come from within, and defile the man" (Mk 7:20-23).

Jesus also said that "out of the abundance of the heart the mouth speaketh" (Mt 12:34). The scribes and Pharisees refused to recognize these concepts. To them, the sin was in the act, but not in the thought. Jesus corrected their faulty thinking in the Sermon on the Mount (Mt 5–7). According to Christ, sin went beyond the act to the attitude. Adultery could be committed in the mind as well on the bed. Anger with malice breaks the sixth commandment as much as plunging a knife into the heart of an enemy. One sin involves the mind; the other involves both the mind and the body; but they are both sin. The after-effects of the action may be greater than those of the intent, but they are still both sin. Man is a sinner, both in his soul and in his body, and God holds him responsible for this.

According to Paul, all unsaved men are under sin (Ro 3:9). All men before God and before men do have equality. They are equally under the penalty of sin, equally under the power of sin, and equally under the presence of sin. They are equally lost! Sin dominates them completely —their past, their present, and their future. Paul said that he was "sold under sin" (Ro 7:14). Sin owned and controlled him; he was its slave. To the Galatians, he wrote, "But the scripture hath concluded all under sin, that the promise by faith of Jesus Christ might be given to them that believe" (Gal 3:22). Man does not see himself in this desperate predicament. He believes that he can control the problems, the weaknesses, and the sins of himself and of society. He does not know that he is actually under the iron-fist rule of sin. When he does see himself as being under sin, he is then a candidate for salvation.

In summary, the Bible depicts man as being morally and spiritually depraved. What does depravity mean? Negatively, it does not mean that man is as bad as he could be. There are sinners who have sinned more and others who have sinned less. There are moral sinners and there are immoral sinners, but they are both sinners before God. No man has ever put into practice the full potential of his sin nature. The restraint of the Holy Spirit, the influence of Christians in the world as salt and light, and the purposes of God have prevented him from doing so. Depravity does not mean that a man does not have any knowledge of God. It does not mean that man does not appreciate the quality of goodness or that he does not do good. Jesus said that evil men could give good gifts unto their children (Lk 11:13).

Positively, depravity means that there is nothing in man that will merit God's approval. There is nothing that man can do to gain acceptance before God. This is God's estimation of man; it is not man's evaluation of himself. It means that in man there is a total absence of holiness "without which no man shall see the Lord" (Heb 12:14). It does not mean that man has achieved the highest intensity of sin in his personal experience.

The sense of depravity is hard to communicate. Whenever men hear the word *depraved,* they immediately think of a corrupt pervert or a sin-cursed soul. However, *depravity* refers to man's position before God, not his practice. He is *as bad off* as he can be, but he is not necessarily *as bad as* he can be. Depravity is true of man's total being —his intellect, his emotion, and his will. There is nothing that he can think, feel, or do, that will produce God's type of righteousness within his life. This is true of every man who has ever lived.

Depravity is seen in Job's question: "Who can bring a clean thing out of an unclean? not one" (Job 14:4). Eliphaz's question is similar: "What is man, that he should be clean? and he which is born of a woman, that he should be righteous" (Job 15:14). David knew that he was "shapen in iniquity" (Ps 51:5), and Solomon observed that there was not a just man upon earth (Ec 7:20).

Man is both dead and dying. His spirit is dead and his body is dying. He is like the criminal in death row, condemned to die in the electric chair, and also afflicted with terminal cancer. He needs a double remedy or a double life. He must be delivered from both the guilt of sin and the corruption of sin's effects upon his body. He is incapable of doing anything to produce this deliverance. Only God can provide the type of redemption that he needs.

Fifth and finally, man is condemned because of his relationship to God. Man could be condemned simply on the basis of his inhumanity to man, his dissipation of his own person, and his pollution of his environment. (Note how ecologists refer to the *sin* of spoiling our biosphere—our air, earth, and water.) Ultimately, however, man stands condemned because of his position before a holy God.

Most men profess to believe in some kind of a god, but it is a god of their own making or one that has been passed down to them through tradition. The Bible actually describes the unsaved man as one who is "without God in the world" (Eph 2:12). He is without God in the fullest sense of the term *God*. He has no claim on God. There is not a single bit of the presence of the genuine, living God in his life. He is truly ungodly or godless, in that there is no vital relationship between himself and the God who created this universe and who provided redemption through Christ.

Paul wrote that "if any man have not the Spirit of Christ, he is none of his" (Ro 8:9). Jude said that one of the characteristics of the unregenerate is "having not the Spirit" (Jude 19). There are two groups of people in the world: those who have the Holy Spirit (the saved) and

those who have not the Spirit (the unsaved). There are
no other possibilities. You cannot have a saved man without the Spirit and you cannot have an unsaved man who
has the Spirit.

John said, "He that hath the Son hath life; and he that
hath not the Son of God hath not life" (1 Jn 5:12). Paul
added that the unsaved man is "without Christ" (Eph
2:12). In Christ is life, the very life of God (Jn 1:4). If a
man does not have Jesus Christ dwelling within his life,
he is an unsaved person. Christ said: "I am the way, the
truth, and the life: no man cometh unto the Father, but by
me" (Jn 14:6). This means that the atheist, the animist,
the Muslim, the Buddhist, and the Christian religionist,
cannot have access to God. He must come only through
Christ.

Man is simply guilty before God. He has broken the
moral law of God, he knows it, and he is liable. Instead of
arguing with God about his sinful violations, the unregenerate man should admit his guilt (Ro 3:20). Man has
no basis of appeal before God. He cannot blame his situation on heredity or environment. He must blame himself.
Read Paul's description of the guilty man:

> As it is written, There is none righteous, no, not one:
> There is none that understandeth, there is none that seek-
> eth after God.
> They are all gone out of the way, they are together be-
> come unprofitable; there is none that doeth good, no, not
> one. Their throat is an open sepulchre; with their tongues
> they have used deceit; the poison of asps is under their
> lips: Whose mouth is full of cursing and bitterness: Their
> feet are swift to shed blood: Destruction and misery are
> in their ways: And the way of peace have they not
> known: There is no fear of God before their eyes (Ro
> 3:10-18).

Is it any wonder men are guilty before God? If man cried out for justice, he would receive eternal condemnation. That is what his position and practice deserve. Instead he should appeal for mercy and grace. He should fall on his knees, asking for forgiveness out of a repentant heart.

This is why God gave the law. He did not give it so that man could keep it and thereby gain eternal life (Gal 3:21). The law is holy, just, and good (Ro 7:12), but because of man's weakness or inability, it could not produce righteousness (Ro 8:3). The law was given so that man could understand God's holy character, recognize his own sinful being, and place his faith in God's provision for his salvation. The law was a mirror so that man could see his moral despair and call upon God for his cleansing.

The Bible places every non-Christian under the wrath of God. "He that believeth on the Son hath everlasting life: and he that believeth not the Son shall not see life; but the wrath of God abideth on him" (Jn 3:36). This is the position of the unregenerate man; however he will not experience God's wrath until after death in hades or hell and later in the lake of fire (Lk 16:19-31; Rev 20:11-15). Until then, the wrath of God hangs over him as the sword of Damocles. Only the thread of a heartbeat keeps him from fully experiencing it. Deliverance is possible, but it must come before physical death. After death, it is too late. Deliverance comes through believing in Christ. You either have everlasting life within you or the wrath of God upon you.

The unsaved man is also without hope (Eph 2:12). What a sad picture! In the hospital, those are heart-wrenching words. When the doctor looks at you and says, "We have given up hope," what pain and remorse that announcement brings. Men have lived on hope. They have survived in concentration or POW camps because they hoped that rescue or release was imminent. But when hope dies or is absent, man can sink to new lows of mental, emotional, and spiritual depression. Man without God is also without hope, both in this life and after death.

Hope is part of faith. Paul wrote:

> For we are saved by hope: but hope that is seen is not hope: for what a man seeth, why doth he yet hope for? But if we hope for that we see not, then do we with patience wait for it (Ro 8:24-25).

The Thessalonians were marked by their work of faith, labor of love, and patience of hope (1 Th 1:3). They had a living hope. They had put their faith in Jesus Christ, the one who was crucified, buried, raised from the dead, ascended into God's presence, and who could come at any moment to take them likewise into God's heaven. The unsaved do not have this hope (1 Th 4:13). God sees them in total despair.

As far as God is concerned, man is lost. He is morally lost in an infinite forest with no spiritual compass. It is a forest in a land of perpetual darkness. He could grope for an eternity and never find a way out. Man cannot rescue himself. God must penetrate that forest and save him, and that is exactly what Christ did. "For the Son of man is come to seek and to save that which was lost" (Lk 19:10). Man is lost and only God through Christ can find him.

To conclude, this chapter has demonstrated why men are unsaved. They are condemned because they have rejected divine revelation. The relationships that they sustain to the world, to Satan, to sin, and to God also make them guilty. Every unsaved man is marked by the biblical characteristics set forth in this chapter, whether he is aware of them or not. Why was this chapter written, and why did I make it the first chapter? Because if a man could lose his spiritual deliverance through Christ, he would have to return fully to his former position and practice. In order to be guilty before God once more, he would have to return to the complete state of the lost man who has never been saved.

When a person says that he has lost his salvation, ask him why. He will usually refer to a terrible sin that he has committed or to a cold feeling in his heart. But, is he doing what the Bible says condemns a person? Does he reject the revelation of God in nature, in his conscience, or in the Bible? Is he still blinded to spiritual truth? These are not true of the genuine Christian, even if he is the worst backslider who has ever lived. It is impossible for a man, once saved, to duplicate his spiritual state of lostness, for which he was condemned.

The question of the psalmist should make more sense now: "What is man, that thou art mindful of him?" (Ps 8:4). The vastness of the universe makes man seem insignificant. The lostness of man makes him appear undesirable to a holy God. But God *is* mindful of man. God has visited man in grace and redemption. In the next chapter, we shall see what a remarkable salvation God has provided at the cross and given us through faith in His Son, Jesus Christ.

2

What Does It Mean to Be Saved?

Saved! saved! saved!
My sins are all forgiv'n;
Christ is mine!
I'm on my way to heav'n;

Once a guilty sinner,
Lost, undone,
Now a child of God,
Saved thro' His Son.

Saved! I'm saved
Thro' Christ, my all in all;
Saved! I'm saved,
Whatever may befall;

He died upon the cross for me,
He bore the awful penalty;
And now I'm saved eternally—
I'm saved! saved! saved!

Oswald J. Smith*

WHAT BEAUTIFUL WORDS Oswald Smith has penned! This was his testimony, and it has also been the singing, ringing testimony of Christians down through the years. "I'm saved!" No more glorious words could ever come out of the mouth of man. It speaks of the joy of deliverance. It is a personal redemption (note the "I"). It is a present pos-

*Copyright by Hope Publishing Co. Used by permission.

session (note the "am"). It is a deliverance (note the "saved") accomplished by someone else, namely Christ.

However, many Christians only have a vague idea as to what their salvation involves. To most, getting saved just means keeping out of hell or just getting into heaven. They only see their salvation in terms of eternal destiny. But salvation is far more than that! Paul wrote, "Blessed be the God and Father of our Lord Jesus Christ, who hath blessed us with all spiritual blessings in heavenly places in Christ" (Eph 1:3). The child of God has already been blessed with all spiritual blessings. It is not that he *will* be blessed in the future or that he *has* received a few divine favors. All blessings are his *now!* That is the message of this verse. These "blessings" do not refer to the daily blessings that God gives to His child who obeys Him and walks in His will. These are the blessings of his position before God as a saved person. They belong to him now, and they are abundant.

When one realizes the guilty, lost condition from which he has been saved and the blessed position to which he has been brought by salvation, then he will better understand the divine purpose behind the program of salvation: "That in the ages to come he [God] might shew the exceeding riches of his grace in his kindness toward us through Christ Jesus" (Eph 2:7). The riches of God's grace can be seen in the spiritual blessings that God has bestowed upon us. Throughout eternity, God will be glorified for what He has done for man.

Scripture reveals about fifty of these spiritual riches, although, doubtless there are more. They could only be known by studying the Bible, because they are not experienced. The joy and peace of salvation are experienced, but these are not. Just as a child cannot remember what happened at the moment of conception or birth, so a child of God must be told what happened at the moment of his salvation. This is why salvation rests upon what God has done, not upon our feelings at the moment it was done for us. These spiritual riches became ours instantaneously at salvation; they are not given to us gradually during our lifetime. They are not given as rewards for faithful Christian living. They are grace gifts, conferred by God apart from any merit within us. They are an integral part of the eternal salvation that God has given, not an accessory or a fringe benefit. They constitute the character of salvation. They are the permanent, eternal possession of the believer. If a person could lose his salvation, then all of these riches would have to be lost or surrendered. Not just a few, but all! Since they were not gained as the result of practice or human merit, so they cannot be forfeited by the lack of practice or lack of human favor. These spiritual riches of divine grace manifest the glorious position of the child of God. They are true of every believer, regardless of whether he is aware of them.

These spiritual truths have been arbitrarily grouped. There is no special significance to their order. Each truth is just as important as another. For convenience of study, they have been arranged into groups that bear a common relationship.

Some spiritual blessings reflect a special relationship to God the Father. God planned the program of salvation in eternity past; it is being executed in our present time-and-space universe; it will be a permanent part of eternity future. The child of God should be aware of God's sovereign purpose for his life. If he is, it will affect his attitudes and behavior.

The Bible states that the believer was foreknown of God (Ro 8:29). God knows everything, both actual and possible. He knows the end from the beginning; He is omniscient. How does this relate to the believer? Does *foreknowledge* simply mean that God knew from eternity that you would one day live and receive Christ? And, how did He know that you would receive Christ if given the opportunity and that another would reject Him, when both of you were in the same desperate spiritual condition? Does *foreknow* simply mean knowledge before the fact? Peter said that Christ "was foreordained [foreknown, Greek] before the foundation of the world, but was manifest in these last times for you" (1 Pe 1:20). On the day of Pentecost, Peter preached these words, "Him [Christ], being delivered by the determinate counsel and foreknowledge of God, ye have taken, and by wicked hands have crucified and slain" (Ac 2:23). Did God only know that one day Christ would come and die on Calvary's cross, or is there something more behind the term? God said to Israel, "You only have I known of all the families of the earth" (Amos 3:2). What does this mean? God surely knew of the existence of other nations, both then and now. But God *chose* Israel and knew Israel in a distinctive way because of His choice and plan for Israel. Choice, determination, and decree, are all involved in the biblical meaning of *foreknowledge*. God's foreknowledge is certain, because it is based upon His decree or His will to act. God foreknew Calvary because He decreed that Christ would die according to His will or counsel. God foreknew Israel because He chose to make of Abraham a great nation through whom He would bless the world. This was done in spite of the fact that God surely knew of Israel's sinful and faithless history. Christians likewise are "elect according to the foreknowledge of God the Father" (1 Pe 1:2). God foreknew you and me because He determined to save us, in spite of our future sins and failures which He also knew since eternity. The eternal plan of foreknowledge for the believer cannot be rescinded any more than that for Israel or for Christ's death. All are eternally certain. "Known unto God are all his works from the beginning of the world" (Ac 15:18).

The believer is not only foreknown, but he is also predestinated by God. Paul argued, "For whom he did foreknow, he also did predestinate to be conformed to the image of his Son, that he might be the firstborn among many brethren" (Ro 8:29). To the Ephesians, he wrote, "Having predestinated us unto the adoption of children by Jesus Christ to himself, according to the good pleasure of his will, To the praise of the glory of his grace" (Eph 1:5-6a). *Predestination* is a greatly misunderstood term and doctrine. It is nowhere used in the Bible to denote a predestination of a person to hell or to heaven. It is a term used only to point out the guaranteed future destiny of the child of God. God has determined that every believer will one day come into the full position of sonship. *Adoption* means "to be put into the position of a son." This will take place at the coming of Christ. Paul said that "we ourselves groan within ourselves, waiting for the adoption, to wit, the redemption of our body" (Ro 8:23). When our mortal, corruptible bodies are changed into immortal, incorruptible bodies, then we will be fully conformed to the image of Christ. John wrote, "Beloved, now are we the sons of God, and it doth not yet appear what we shall be: but we know that, when he shall appear, we shall be like him; for we shall see him as he is"(1 Jn 3:2). *Predestination* means that we shall be like Him. Within God's decree, it is certain; "he *did* predestinate"—note the tense; time awaits the fullfillment in our experience. The standard of divine predestination is the good pleasure of God's will. The ultimate goal of this decree is the glorification of His grace. Since grace (the giving of God's favor apart from human merit) involves predestination, the goal of predestination rests not upon the faithfulness of the believer, but rather upon the certainty of God's will.

The believer is also designated as *elect* and *chosen*. Jesus said to his disciples: "Ye have not chosen me, but I have chosen you" (Jn 15:16). They did not originate the choice; He did. He chose them out of the world of lost, guilty sinners (Jn 15:19). This choice was made in eternity past. Note Paul's words, "According as he [God] hath chosen us in him before the foundation of the world, that we should be holy and without blame before him in love" (Eph 1:4). The purpose of God's choice was our perfect standing. Negatively, we are without blame; our sins have been forgiven and the guilt of our sin has been pardoned. Positively, we are holy in position because we are completely covered by Christ's righteousness. As God's elect, no one can condemn us, because our position is secure (Ro 8:33-34). Our election is according to God's foreknowledge (1 Pe 1:2). Our election to salvation is based upon the same principle as God's choice of Jacob through whom the blessings of the Abrahamic covenant would come to the world. Paul wrote,

> And not only this; but when Rebecca also had conceived by one, even by our father Isaac; (For the children being not yet born, neither having done any good or evil, that the purpose of God according to election might stand, not of works, but of him that calleth;) It was said unto her, The elder shall serve the younger. As it is written, Jacob have I loved, but Esau have I hated (Ro 9:10-13).

It cannot be said that God knew that Jacob would be more spiritual than Esau, and that on the basis of that knowledge, He chose Jacob. God chose Jacob simply because it was His will to do so. It was not on the basis of human works. If it were, Jacob would hardly have been chosen.

His life was full of lies and deception. The election of God is appropriated by faith (Titus 1:1), is made evident by the outward signs of a conversion experience (1 Th 1:3-7), and should issue in a change of moral character and behavior (Col 3:12-17). Christ is also called "the elect of God" (1 Pe 2:4). The fact and the fulfillment of the election of believers are just as sure as His.

The believer is also called of God. To all men, God has issued a general call to salvation, as Jesus said in the conclusion of the parable of the marriage feast: "For many are called, but few are chosen" (Mt 22:14). God has invited all men to the blessings of salvation through Christ. He is "not willing that any should perish, but that all should come to repentance" (2 Pe 3:9). Every believer is under obligation to pray for all men and to witness to all men:

> For this is good and acceptable in the sight of God our Saviour; Who will have all men to be saved, and to come unto the knowledge of the truth. For there is one God, and one mediator between God and men, the man Christ Jesus; Who gave himself a ransom for all, to be testified in due time, (1 Ti 2:3-6).

This general call is an expression of divine grace. It alone does not save nor does it always lead to salvation. Man must respond to this call. Paul wrote, "For whosoever shall call upon the name of the Lord shall be saved" (Ro 10:13). However, not every man answers God's general call by calling upon Him. Many are called, but few are chosen. The chosen are those who are the objects of God's *effectual* call. They are the called ones according to God's eternal purpose (Ro 8:28). It is God's direct will that these called receive all that is involved in God's gift of salvation. Note Paul's words, "Moreover whom he did predestinate, them he also called: and whom he called, them he also justified:

and whom he justified, them he also glorified" (Ro 8:30). These called have already (according to God's sovereign decree) been foreknown and predestinated. Their justification and glorification are just as certain as their calling. The saved are those who have responded by faith to both God's eternal and effectual call. The unsaved reject God's general call. Because of the greatness of God's effectual call, Paul exhorted the Christians of his day and of ours to "walk worthy of the vocation [calling, Greek] wherewith ye are called" (Eph 4:1). The child of God can have confidence that God will complete the purpose of His divine call because of His faithfulness—the faithfulness of His character and His faithfulness to His Word (1 Th 5:24).

When a person receives Jesus Christ by faith, he also receives the gift of God's righteousness (Ro 3:22). He is made righteous by God. Paul wrote: "But of him are ye in Christ Jesus, who of God is made unto us . . . righteousness" (1 Co 1:30). Paul wanted to be "found in him [Christ], not having mine own righteousness, which is of the law, but that which is through the faith of Christ, the righteousness which is of God by faith" (Phil 3:9). Just as Jesus Christ, who neither knew nor did any sin, was made sin on the cross of Calvary for us, so we, who neither knew nor did any righteousness, were made righteous at the moment of faith (2 Co 5:21). We have no righteousness of our own (Ro 3:10); but through Christ we are not only given God's righteousness, but we are made righteous. In position and standing, we are just as righteous as Christ. In practice, we are not as righteous or holy as we should be. Compare this truth with what Christ did on the cross. In practice, He never sinned; but positionally, He became just as sinful as we are when the wrath of God came upon Him and when He was forsaken of the Father during those last three hours of darkness. That event cannot be reversed or repeated. Christ can never return to a position He held before Calvary (to an unslain Lamb position); nor does He have to die again. So it is with the child of God. The event of the imputation of righteousness to him cannot be reversed or repeated.

After a sinner has been made righteous through faith in Jesus Christ, he is then justified by God. This is the logical order. *Justify* means "to declare righteous." God can only declare righteous those who really are righteous. He cannot justify a sinner per se; He can and does justify sinners who have been made righteous in Christ. Some say that God looks at the justified person as if he had never sinned, but that is only one half of the truth. The believer has been forgiven of his sin and guilt, but that only makes him innocent. He needs to be made righteous also in order for God to declare him righteous. He needs the positive side of imputation as well as the negative.

The Bible describes justification in a sevenfold fashion. A justified position is a grace gift (Ro 3:24). Only a just God could be its source (Ro 3:26). The righteous position is appropriated by faith and brings peace between God and man (Ro 3:28; 5:1). It is made possible only upon the foundation of the shed blood of Christ (Ro 5:9). Only in Christ can one have a justified position (1 Co 6:11). This work of God is applied to the believing sinner by the Holy Spirit (1 Co 6:11). The outward manifestation of the justified position is a changed life, marked by the works that genuine faith produces (Ja 2:21-26). John beautifully described the justified person with these words, "Herein is our love made perfect, that we may have boldness in the day of judgment: because as he is, so are we in this world" (1 Jn 4:17). Every person should want to have boldness of speech and to be free of anxiety when he stands before God's judgment throne. The believer has

it. "As he is, so are we." Just as Christ is (in heaven), so
are we (in this world). He is accepted before God; so we
are, because we are in Him, righteous and declared righteous. In other words, we are as good as Christ is, in our
spiritual position. If we could lose our position before God
in this world, then potentially, Christ could lose His too.
Both are impossible. No wonder Paul shouted, "Who shall
lay anything to the charge of God's elect? It is God that
justifieth" (Ro 8:33). The law of double jeopardy states
that a man cannot be tried or punished twice for the same
crime. The believer will not be tried or punished either,
because he has already been declared righteous by God.
Christ was punished for his crime. God cannot and will
not require a double punishment for our sin.

The sinner has also been reconciled to God and by God.
Paul wrote,

> And all things are of God, who hath reconciled us to
> himself by Jesus Christ, and hath given to us the ministry
> of reconciliation; To wit, that God was in Christ, reconcil-
> ing the world unto himself, not imputing their trespasses
> unto them; and hath committed unto us the word of rec-
> onciliation. Now then we are ambassadors for Christ, as
> though God did beseech you by us: we pray you in
> Christ's stead, be ye reconciled to God (2 Co 5:18-20).

Man was God's enemy; God was not man's enemy. Sin
estranged man from God. Adam went into hiding, not
God. Reconciliation is man-ward, not God-ward; it is a
one-way street. Calvary made possible a reconciliation,
"For if, when we were enemies, we were reconciled to God
by the death of his Son, much more, being reconciled, we
shall be saved by his life" (Ro 5:10). The resurrection of
Christ guarantees the permanence of the reconciled position. If Christ did so much for us when we were the
enemies of God, just imagine what He can do for us now

that we are His children! Reconciliation has provided a way back for the sinner to God and for a sinning Christian to his Father (a double value and purpose). Reconciliation gives access by the removal of the sin barrier. Paul said,

> And that he might reconcile both unto God in one body by the cross, having slain the enmity thereby: And came and preached peace to you which were afar off, and to them that were nigh. For through him we both have access by one Spirit unto the Father (Eph 2:16-18).

To lose reconciliation, the enmity would have to be resurrected and the access turned into prohibition.

It is said of the believer that he has been made nigh: "But now in Christ Jesus ye who sometimes were far off are made nigh by the blood of Christ" (Eph 2:13). This is especially true of Gentile Christians. In their racial heritage, they were "aliens from the commonwealth of Israel," "strangers from the covenants of promise," "far off," and "foreigners" (Eph 2:12, 13, 19). Positionally, the Gentile sinner was once far from God, but now he is near. Practically, he is exhorted: "Draw nigh to God, and he will draw nigh to you" (Ja 4:8). A husband and a wife can live under the same roof and still be miles apart in their love relationship. Likewise, a Christian can be practically far away from God even though his position is near. We are *made* nigh positionally; we *draw* nigh in our daily experience.

Related to nearness is the fact that the believer has access to God. He has access by saving faith in Jesus Christ: "By whom also we have access by faith into this grace wherein we stand, and rejoice in hope of the glory of God" (Ro 5:2). He has gained access into a grace position or standing, not of his own doing, but of His giving. He can rejoice because this access was gained and is maintained by God's grace, and is not dependent upon his merit, either past or present. He also has access by the Holy Spirit: "For through him we both have access by one Spirit unto the Father" (Eph 2:18). This access assures the believer that at any time for any reason he can come before God. The door is always open before him. In ancient kings' courts, one would not dare to enter into the king's presence without being called first (Est 4:11). In Israel, men were shut out of the direct presence of God in the holy of holies (both in the tabernacle and in the temple) by the inner veil. The high priest gained admission into that sacred place only once a year on the Day of Atonement, and then he stayed just briefly. But God's presence is ever open to the believer.

> Having therefore, brethren, boldness to enter into the holiest by the blood of Jesus,
> By a new and living way, which he hath consecrated for us, through the veil, that is to say, his flesh;
> And having an high priest over the house of God;
> Let us draw near with a true heart in full assurance of faith, having our hearts sprinkled from an evil conscience, and our bodies washed with pure water (Heb 10:19-22).

Mercy and grace are ever available to the believer.

The Christian is known as a son of God. He becomes a son by adoption. The Greek word for adoption means "to place into the position of sonship." Do not think of this in the natural, human order of adoption wherein a child, a genetic outsider, can become a legal member of another family. A person receives the nature of God, eternal life, at the moment of saving faith, and thereby becomes a child of God. At that same instant, God puts His child into the position of sonship. God regards him as an adult son, with all of the privileges and responsibilities pertaining to maturity. This means that a person does not have to be saved five, ten, or twenty-one years before he can enjoy his spiritual privileges or discharge his spiritual responsibilities. The young Christian (saved one hour) has the same claim on the blessings of God as the old Christian (saved thirty years), and he has the same responsibility to obey God's word. Paul wrote: "For as many as are led by the Spirit of God, they are the sons of God. For ye have not received the spirit of bondage again to fear; but ye have received the Spirit of adoption, whereby we cry, Abba, Father" (Ro 8:14-15). Adoption is based upon redemption (Gal 4:5). It permits a believer to receive by inheritance all that our rich heavenly Father has willed to us: "Wherefore thou art no more a servant, but a son; and if a son, then an heir of God through Christ" (Gal 4:7). We are fellow-heirs with Christ (Ro 8:17) because of our identification with Him in His death, burial, and resurrection. The fullness of our adoption will take place at the redemption of our bodies (Ro 8:23). Adoption is also a goal of God's predestination for us (Eph 1:5). The sonship of the believer is as secure as the eternal purposes of God.

To many, salvation is merely man-centered (anthropocentric). But did only man gain when he believed? No, God gained something too! The Christian is called His inheritance. Paul prayed that the Ephesians might know "what is the hope of his calling, and what the riches of the glory of his inheritance in the saints" are (Eph 1:18). God gained you and me when He saved us. If we could somehow lose our salvation, God would be the greater loser. He would have lost part of His inheritance, and Satan would chuckle and gloat over his seizure of what belonged to God throughout eternity. God will never surrender what belongs to Him by right of creation or redemption.

God has also glorified the believer. At first, this sounds ridiculous because the believer does not have his glorified body yet. But God calls "those things which be not as though they were" (Ro 4:17). He called Abraham a father of many nations even before Abraham had his first son. He regards us as glorified, even though Christ has not yet come and our bodies are still mortal and corruptible. God's eternal purposes are a present reality and certainty to Him. Glorification is the climax of His eternal purpose for us.

> And we know that all things work together for good to them that love God, to them who are the called according to his purpose. For whom he did foreknow, he also did predestinate to be conformed to the image of his Son, that he might be the firstborn among many brethren. Moreover whom he did predestinate, them he also called: and whom he called, them he also justified: and whom he justified, them he also glorified (Ro 8:28-30).

As far as God is concerned, we are as good as glorified. Positionally, we are glorified, because we are in Christ, and Christ is in heaven in a glorified state. If we could lose our glorification, then Christ would have to lose His. Paul reckoned "that the sufferings of this present time are not worthy to be compared with the glory which shall be revealed in us" (Ro 8:18). The deliverance of the Christian is just as certain as the deliverance of creation from the curse (Ro 8:19-22). Both rest upon God's sovereign purpose. Our glorified position will become a living reality to us when Christ comes. "For ye are dead, and your life is hid with Christ in God. When Christ, who is our life, shall appear, then shall ye also appear with him in glory" (Col 3:3-4).

This next truth is absolutely fantastic. The Bible states that the believer is in God and that God is in the believer. To be in God is our position; God in us is our possession, our privilege, and our power. The believer is in God the Father (1 Th 1:1); in God the Son, Jesus Christ (Ro 8:1);

and in God the Holy Spirit (Ro 8:9). That is our spiritual position. Every believer is indwelt by the Father (Eph 4:6), by the Son (Jn 14:20), and by the Spirit (1 Co 6:19). Here is a truth that definitely illustrates Paul's declaration to the Corinthians: "Eye hath not seen, nor ear heard, neither have entered into the heart of man, the things which God hath prepared for them that love him. But God hath revealed them unto us by his Spirit" (1 Co 2:9-10a). How could a finite, sinful person ever be joined in union with an infinite, holy God? The natural man would call this an impossibility, but God says that it can take place. The union of believers to one another and to the persons of the Godhead is similar to the union of the divine persons within the Godhead. Jesus prayed, "That they all may be one; as thou, Father, art in me, and I in thee, that they also may be one in us" (Jn 17:21). The union or one-ness between the believer and God can no more be broken than the oneness that exists between the Son and the Father. It is a secure and eternal union.

These blessings just discussed reveal the special relation-ship between the believer and the Father. The Bible also describes a unique relationship that exists between every Christian and God the Son, our Saviour Jesus Christ. This does not mean that the Father is totally absent from this second relationship; it only means that the emphasis or focus is switched to the Son. Now that you have believed, what special positions or titles do you possess before the Saviour?

Paul wrote that God "hath made us accepted in the be-loved" (Eph 1:6). Jesus Christ is the beloved one (Mt 3:17). A sinner does not make himself acceptable to God, either in the past or in the present, by his deeds. He is *made* acceptable by someone else, namely by God. His sphere of acceptance is *in* the beloved Christ. Apart from our position in Christ, we have no acceptable standing before God (1 Pe 2:5). The poet was correct when he wrote:

> Nearer, nearer, nearer to God
> I cannot be;
> For in the person of His Son,
> I am as near as He.
>
> Dearer, dearer, dearer to God
> I cannot be;
> For in the person of His Son,
> I am as dear as He.
>
> AUTHOR UNKNOWN

This is why Paul wanted to be found in Christ (Phil 3:9), because only in Christ could he find an acceptable, righteous standing. Our acceptance by God, therefore, is not based upon our practice, either before or after saving faith, but rather upon our position in Christ.

The believer is now a citizen of Christ's spiritual kingdom. Paul wrote: "Who [God] hath delivered us from the power of darkness, and hath translated us into the kingdom of his dear Son" (Col 1:13). This verse gives both a negative and a positive truth. The believing sinner has been delivered *from* satanic dominion, but he has also been removed *into* the kingdom of the Son of His love. Salvation is both *from* and *to*. This change of personal rulership has already taken place. Note the tense of "translated." This is an everlasting kingdom (2 Pe 1:11); therefore, Christ's dominion over the believer is an everlasting dominion. There is no mention of the possibility of a translation back to the dominion of Satan. Believers have been called unto Christ's kingdom and glory (1 Th 2:12). The certainty of this call rests upon the faithfulness of God to His Word (1 Th 5:24).

In His conclusion to the Sermon on the Mount, Jesus

gave the story of two houses and two foundations (Mt 7:24-27). One house was built upon a rock; the other was built upon sand. The rock represented Christ and His righteousness; the sand represented the scribes and Pharisees and their type of righteousness. The houses represent people and their decisions. A life that is founded upon Christ (hearing His sayings and doing them) cannot be destroyed by the storms of circumstance; a life that is constructed upon the pride and effort of man will fall. The foundation determines the security of the house, not vice versa. The believer is built upon the foundation of Jesus Christ. Paul elaborated this truth to the Corinthians:

> For we are labourers together with God: ye are God's husbandry, ye are God's building. According to the grace of God which is given unto me, as a wise masterbuilder, I have laid the foundation, and another buildeth thereon. But let every man take heed how he buildeth thereupon. For other foundation can no man lay than that is laid which is Jesus Christ (1 Co 3:9-11).

Nothing can be added to the foundation to make it more secure. Salvation is based upon the foundation. The foundation is the person—"Thou art the Christ, the Son of the living God" (Mt 16:16)—and redemptive work of Jesus Christ—His death, burial, and resurrection. The Christian life, then, is built upon this foundation. It can be either a precious or a wasted life. Even if it is a wasted life, practically devoid of anything that God could reward, it is still a saved life because the foundation is solid (1 Co 3:12-15). Loss of salvation would have to come from the removal of the foundation, not from the faulty construction of a life.

A believer is a gift from the Father to the Son. What a marvelous, yet strange, designation of the child of God. In His great prayer of intercession, Jesus used this title for

Christians seven times (Jn 17:2, 6 [twice], 9, 11, 12, 24). Every believer belongs to the Father and to the Son: "For they are thine. And all mine are thine, and thine are mine" (Jn 17:9c-10a). Eternal life is given to those who were given to the Son by the Father (Jn 17:2). The believer was given out of the world to the Son by the Father (Jn 17:6). Such a believer keeps God's Word (Jn 17:6). These gifted ones are the objects of Christ's prayer (Jn 17:9) both for preservation (Jn 17:11) and for eternal habitation (Jn 17:24). When was the believer given by the Father to the Son? The Scripture is not definite here, perhaps in eternity past as part of the eternal purpose of God, perhaps at Calvary, or at the time of one's personal salvation. In any case, Christ viewed them as belonging to Him, not because they had believed on Him, but because the Father had given them to Him.

At Corinth, God encouraged Paul in his preaching with these words: "Be not afraid, but speak, and hold not thy peace: For I am with thee, and no man shall set on thee to hurt thee: for I have much people in this city" (Ac 18:9-10). A great security passage is introduced with this concept: "My Father, which gave them me, is greater than all; and no man is able to pluck them out of my Father's hand" (Jn 10:29). If Christians could lose their salvation, the Father would have to take back those whom He had given to the Son; but even then, the Father would still have them. But why should the Father take back those whom He had given to Christ? Has Christ been unfaithful to the extent that God takes away this gift from Him? Impossible! Every believer is an eternal gift to the Son.

Paul wrote to the Colossians: "In whom also ye are circumcised with the circumcision made without hands, in putting off the body of the sins of the flesh by the circumcision of Christ" (Col 2:11). A believer is circumcised in Christ. Let us make a distinction between physical and spiritual circumcision. Physical circumcision was instituted by God as an outward sign of the Abrahamic covenant (Gen 17:9-14). Eight days after birth, Jewish parents circumcised their male children in obedience and as a sign of their faith in the fulfillment of the covenant promises. Circumcision became the mark of distinction between a Jew and a Gentile (Eph 2:11). Many Jews trusted in their circumcision for their salvation, but Paul criticized this false concept:

> For he is not a Jew, which is one outwardly; neither is that circumcision, which is outward in the flesh: But he is a Jew, which is one inwardly; and circumcision is that of the heart, in the spirit, and not in the letter; whose praise is not of men, but of God (Ro 2:28-29).

A true Israelite is one who has a double circumcision. The outward sign relates him to Abraham as his physical father; the inward, heart circumcision relates him to Abraham as his spiritual father. Paul said, "For we are the circumcision, which worship God in the spirit, and rejoice in Christ Jesus, and have no confidence in the flesh" (Phil 3:3). The "body of the sins of the flesh" has been removed, positionally, once and for all from the converted sinner. The rite of physical circumcision cannot be reversed or repeated; it is a natural impossibility. The reality of spiritual circumcision also cannot be repeated or reversed. It is a spiritual impossibility.

The believer is also a member of the body of Christ. Paul revealed this organic, living relationship between Christ, the head, and Christians, the body, thus: "So we, being many, are one body in Christ, and every one members one of another" (Ro 12:5; cf. 1 Co 12:12; Eph 4:4). When Jesus Christ ascended into heaven, He then became

"head over all things to the church, which is his body"
(Eph 1:22-23). This headship is equivalent to and illustrated by the headship of the husband in the home (Eph
5:22-33). Paul aptly describes the relationship:

> So ought men to love their wives as their own bodies.
> He that loveth his wife loveth himself. For no man ever
> yet hated his own flesh; but nourisheth and cherisheth it,
> even as the Lord of the church: For we are members of
> his body, of his flesh, and of his bones (Eph 5:28-30).

A Christian is a member of Christ's body, a member of
His flesh, and a member of His bones. Would Christ ever
hate one of His members? Never. Rather, He loves,
nourishes, and cherishes every single member. Could
Christ's body be dismembered? Absolutely impossible. If
a Christian could lose his salvation, then Christ's body
would be less than complete. It would be scarred or dis-
figured. Every believer is organically related to Him; he is
a part of Christ's spiritual body, the church.

The Christian has also been baptized into Christ. Spirit
baptism, not water baptism, accomplishes this identification at the moment of salvation. Paul wrote, "Buried with
him in baptism, wherein also ye are risen with him through
the faith of the operation of God, who hath raised him
from the dead" (Col 2:12; cf. Ro 6:3-4). Just as the unsaved man sinned in Adam (Ro 5:12), so the saved man
died in Christ, was buried in Christ, and was raised in
Christ. The Bible teaches the cocrucifixion and coresur-
rection of the believer with Jesus Christ. God reckons His
death to be yours and His resurrection to be yours. Just as
sin and death no longer have dominion over Him, neither
do they have dominion over the believer. Christ cannot
lose the reality and effects of His death and resurrection;
that event cannot be reversed or repeated. Since we were
in Him, neither can our salvation-identification be reversed

or repeated. That is why Paul wrote these famous words, "I am crucified with Christ: nevertheless I live; yet not I, but Christ liveth in me: and the life which I now live in the flesh I live by the faith of the Son of God, who loved me, and gave himself for me" (Gal 2:20).

The believer's relationship to Jesus Christ, God the Son, can be summed up with these words: *complete in Him.* Paul wrote: "For in him [Christ] dwelleth all the fulness of the Godhead bodily. And ye are complete in him, which is the head of all principality and power" (Col 2:9-10). The words *fulness* and *complete* are based on the same Greek word stem. In both His earthly and resurrection body, Jesus Christ was fully God. The perfection of the divine essence or nature has always been in Him. He could never be less divine nor more divine. So it is with the believer. He has reached a state of completion or perfection in his position in Christ that can neither be improved nor weakened. Positionally, he can never be more acceptable than he is right now. He did not reach this state of completion by good works. He has been made complete by God, and He rests in that standing of completion before a holy and just God.

The Christian also maintains a unique relationship to the third Person of the Godhead, the Holy Spirit. The Spirit applies the plan of the Father and the redemptive work of the Son to the believer. He also protects and guarantees the secured salvation.

First of all, the child of God has been born again or begotten of the Spirit. Jesus said that a man had to be born again in order to see and to enter the kingdom of God (both the spiritual and the millennial kingdoms). When Nicodemus raised the question of the method of such a birth, Jesus replied, "That which is born of the flesh is flesh; and that which is born of the Spirit is spirit" (Jn 3:6;

cf. 3:5, 8). There is a difference between natural birth
and spiritual birth. Natural birth gives natural life; spiritual birth gives spiritual life. Peter wrote that the Christian is "born again, not of corruptible seed, but of incorruptible, by the word of God, which liveth and abideth
for ever" (1 Pe 1:23). The Holy Spirit, or the incorruptible seed, is the source of the new birth (*of* from *ek*, Greek).
The Word of God, the Bible, is the means by which the
Spirit effects the new birth (*by*, from *dia*).

Men *become* children of God; they are not born that
way (Jn 1:12). They are not automatically Christians because their parents were ("not of blood"; Jn 1:13), because they themselves decided to become such ("nor of
the will of the flesh"; Jn 1:13), or because somebody desired them to become that ("nor of the will of man"; Jn 1-
13). A man must be born of God in order to become a
child of God and to receive the divine nature or eternal life.
Like begets like. An eternal God begets eternal children.
In the human family, conception and birth are not based
upon the will of the fetus, but upon the will of the parents.
Spiritual birth is not based upon the will or effort of man,
but rather upon the will of God. The birth event cannot be
reversed or repeated. A father may disown or disinherit his
son legally, but he cannot remove the fact that his nature is
in his son. The son may not enjoy the blessings of sonship,
but he is still a natural son. The spiritual birth event cannot be reversed or repeated either. What is born remains
born. That is the sense of the Greek: "so is everyone that
is born of the Spirit" (Jn 3:8).

A person is born into God's family by the Spirit at the
time of receiving Christ by faith. He remains in a "born
state" forever. Just as it is impossible for a grown man to
go back into his mother's womb to be born all over, so it is
impossible for a Christian to go back into the "womb" of
the Holy Spirit and be born spiritually a second time.

Closely related to the new birth is the fact that the believer has been washed in regeneration. Paul wrote, "Not by works of righteousness which we have done, but according to his mercy he saved us, by the washing of regeneration, and renewing of the Holy Ghost" (Titus 3:5). The filth and guilt of the sinner must be removed before the pure robe of divine righteousness can be put on. Regeneration not only secures the new birth, but cleanses the sinner. This is a once-for-all cleansing. It cannot be repeated. Paul told the sinning, carnal Corinthian Christians, "Ye are [*were*, Greek] washed . . . by the Spirit of our God" (1 Co 6:11). When Jesus washed the feet of the twelve disciples in the upper room the night before His crucifixion, He said, "He that is washed [*leloumenos*] needeth not save to wash [*nipsasthai*] his feet, but is clean [*katharos*] every whit: and ye are clean [*katharoi*], but not all" (Jn 13:10). Jesus was making a play on words here. Note the different Greek words for *wash* and *clean*. He had just told Peter that washing of the feet was necessary in order to have fellowship with Him (Jn 13:8). To this, Peter requested a bath for the entire body (Jn 13:9). Jesus said that in order to have fellowship with Him, one does not need to repeat the complete bath of regeneration. (The same word is used in Jn 13:10 as in 1 Co 6:11 and Titus 3:5). He only needs to have daily cleansings of his soul that becomes dirty by walking in a sin-cursed world. That is why Jesus declared that *eleven* of them were clean (saved through the complete bath of regeneration), but not Judas (who never experienced regeneration). The need of sinning, carnal Christians is not to be regenerated all over again, but to experience the daily cleansing through confession of known sin (1 Jn 1:9).

The Christian has also been baptized in the Holy Spirit. Paul wrote, "For by [in] one Spirit are we all baptized into

one body, whether we be Jews or Gentiles, whether we be
bond or free; and have been all made to drink into one
Spirit" (1 Co 12:13). The believer has been permanently
immersed in the Spirit and is forever enveloped by Him.
At the same time, he has drunk of the Spirit; therefore, the
Holy Spirit is in him. The believer is not only identified
with the Spirit but with other Christians who likewise are
in the Spirit. They become one in the Spirit and thus are
able to function within the body of Christ, the true church.
Jesus predicted the baptism in the Holy Spirit during His
forty days of postresurrection ministry (Ac 1:5). The
disciples experienced this baptism on the day of Pentecost
when the Spirit, as a wind, "filled all the house where they
were sitting" (Ac 2:2). They were truly immersed in the
Spirit. There is no indication in Scripture that a believer
can lose his baptized position in the Holy Spirit.

To every believer has been given the earnest of the
Spirit. He is in the hearts of believers (2 Co 1:22). He is
the earnest of the Christian's inheritance "until the redemption of the purchased possession" (Eph 1:14). What
does *earnest* mean? In Bible times, it was used as a part
payment in advance for security, as a first installment, and
even as an engagement ring. The earnest is the pledge of
God's intention. It is God's promise to us that He will continue to give and to love until we have received all that
He has planned to give to us. Christians have "the firstfruits of the Spirit" (Ro 8:23). The full harvest or reception of the inheritance will not come until the resurrection
of the Christian dead at the coming of Christ. God, unlike
man, will not break off the engagement. The indwelling
presence of the Holy Spirit in the life of the believer is a
guarantee that a believer will receive all that God has provided. The pledge of the earnest is based upon God's
faithfulness, not upon ours.

Closely linked with the earnest is the fact that God has sealed His children with the Holy Spirit of promise (2 Co 1:22; cf. Eph 1:14). Chronologically, it takes place at the time of saving faith; logically, it follows faith (Eph 1:14). A believer is sealed "unto the day of redemption" (Eph 4:30). The Spirit is the seal. A seal is a sign of ownership and authority. God has stamped or branded us with the Holy Spirit. His indwelling presence is the sign that we belong to Him and that we are under His authority. Paul wrote, "Nevertheless the foundation of God standeth sure, having this seal, The Lord knoweth them that are his. And, Let every one that nameth the name of Christ depart from iniquity" (2 Ti 2:19). How does God know who are His? He can tell by whether the Spirit is present in the life. If the Spirit is present, there will likewise be some departure from sin in the daily experience.

Simply put, the believer has received the Holy Spirit as a gift from God. His presence causes the believer's body to become a holy temple (1 Co 6:19). He enables the believer to comprehend spiritual truth in the Scripture for the first time (1 Co 2:12). He motivates the Christian to love God in gratitude (Ro 5:5). He causes the child of God to cry out "Father" toward heaven (Gal 4:6). He creates within the believer that inner conviction that he truly is born again (1 Jn 3:23; 4:13). If a person does not have the Spirit of God within his life, he is not a Christian (Ro 8:9).

The child of God has been released from a relationship which he once had to Satan. At our conversion, God "delivered us from the power of darkness" (Col 1:13). Satan's grip over the unsaved, as described in the last chapter, is formidable and awesome. Paul saw his missionary responsibility in these words, "To open their eyes, and to turn them from darkness to light, and from the power of Satan

unto God" (Ac 26:18). Read again about Satan's power
in Ephesians 6:12. No one could ever release himself or
escape from such power. No man is capable of such a task.
God, and God alone through Christ, could do it, and He
has done just that.

In his lost condition, man was under sin—under its penalty, power, and presence. In describing man's salvation,
the Bible often uses terms to show what man's present relationship to sin is. To the child of God, these truths are
precious.

> Redeemed, redeemed!
> Redeemed by the blood of the Lamb;
> Redeemed, redeemed,
> His child, and forever, I am.

These words by the blind composer, Fanny Crosby, have
been sung by millions. It is the testimony of the saved. A
Christian is a redeemed person. How can he keep from
singing and talking about it? The Bible pictures the lost
man as a slave to sin. He is owned by it and bound to it.
Redemption, then, is an appropriate word for salvation.
What could redeem man? Certainly not corruptible things
as silver and gold. Man could only be redeemed "with the
precious blood of Christ, as of a lamb without blemish and
without spot" (1 Pe 1:19). Redemption is in Christ alone
(Ro 3:24; cf. Eph 1:7). Christ provided the ransom payment. He bought us; He paid the price with the infinite,
eternal value of His shed blood. He bought us *out* of the
marketplace of sin, and we now belong to Him by right of
purchase. For us to return to such bondage, He would
have to sell us back. Impossible. He has made us free
(Jn 8:36; cf. Gal 5:1). We are free from the hold of sin!
How could a Christian lose his salvation? Is there any
price that Satan could pay to buy us back into his control?
Could we somehow loose ourselves from divine ownership

by the payment of some price? Never. It took the blood of God's own Son to redeem us. That payment cannot be matched. We are His forever.

Jesus Christ is the propitiation for the sins of the believer. John wrote, "And he is the propitiation for our sins: and not for our's only, but also for the sins of the whole world" (1 Jn 2:2). God has accepted Christ as our propitiation (Ro 3:25). His death on the cross has satisfied God's demands for all of our sins—past, present, and future. When the blood was sprinkled on the mercy seat in the most holy place within the tabernacle, God was satisfied, and Israel was spared to another Day of Atonement. Christ's blood is of infinitely more value than animal blood. His death satisfied God forever. The believer knows that the eternal penalty for all of his sins has been canceled because of Christ.

The Christian has been forgiven of his sins. Paul said that "all trespasses" had been forgiven (Col 2:13). According to him, in Christ we have "the forgiveness of sins, according to the riches of his grace" (Eph 1:7). Forgiveness is a present possession. The standard of forgiveness is the wealth of God's grace. Note that it is "according to" and not "out of." If a multimillionaire would give fifty dollars to a Christian college building fund or to a missionary hospital project, he would be giving *out of* his riches. If, instead, he would send a signed blank check, then he would be giving *according to* his wealth.

How many sins do you have? Regardless of whether they are many or few, great or small, God has enough grace to cover and to remove your sins. Paul was a blasphemer of Christ, a persecutor of Christians, and an injurious person; yet God saved him and forgave him (1 Ti 1:13). If God could save Paul, the chief of sinners, then

He can forgive anyone (1 Ti 1:15). Paul wrote to the Corinthians,

> Be not deceived: neither fornicators, nor idolaters, nor
> adulterers, nor effeminate, nor abusers of themselves with
> mankind, Nor thieves, nor covetous, nor drunkards, nor
> revilers, nor extortioners, shall inherit the kingdom of
> God (1 Co 6:9-10).

What a list of terrible sins and sinners, and yet Paul added:
"And such were some of you" (1 Co 6:11). Yes, God can
forgive the worst sins of immorality. His riches of grace
are inexhaustible.

Because the sinner has been forgiven, he should likewise
forgive. Paul wrote, "And be ye kind one to another, ten-
derhearted, forgiving one another, even as God for Christ's
sake hath forgiven you" (Eph 4:32; cf. Col 3:13). We
cannot out-forgive God. If He has forgiven us so much,
should we not forgive so little?

There is a difference between judicial and daily forgiveness. It is comparable to the once-for-all bath of regeneration and the daily cleansings of the believer's walk. The
forgiveness of sins, at the moment of believing faith, gives
the new child of God a proper relationship to or an acceptable standing before God. Daily forgiveness is necessary to maintain fellowship with the Father and to enjoy
the daily blessings of the Father-son relationship. When a
child of God sins, he needs restoration, not a new regeneration. Daily forgiveness is obtained through daily confession. "If we confess our sins, he is faithful and just to
forgive us our sins, and to cleanse us from all unrighteousness" (1 Jn 1:9). Daily sin will make the Christian feel bad
or ashamed, but he will not sense the concept of guilt or
liability to eternal punishment. He has been forgiven all
of his sins judicially by God.

The Christian is now free from the law. He is no longer

under law, but under grace. Paul wrote, "For sin shall not have dominion over you: for ye are not under the law, but under grace" (Ro 6:14). Sin's dominion was through the law: "The sting of death is sin; and the strength of sin is the law" (1 Co 15:56). Man's inability to keep the law manifested his sin and brought him under the curse of the broken law (Ro 7:7-10). A man must keep all the law all of the time in order to escape the penalty of violation. No man could do this; therefore he was under the dominion and penalty of the law and of sin. Christ did something about this problem. He has "redeemed us from the curse of the law, being made a curse for us" (Gal 3:13). He redeemed "them that were under the law, that we might receive the adoption of sons" (Gal 4:5). Men were kept under the law, the schoolmaster (Gal 3:23-25). Faith in Christ releases one from his obligation to a broken law and from any further obligation to keep it. The believer finds favor before God, not through conformity to the Mosaic law, but through conformity to Christ. The law is a minisstration of death, then and always (2 Co 3:7). A believer is "dead to the law" and "delivered from the law" in his new position in Christ (Ro 7:4, 6). Just as a woman is no longer under the law or dominion of the husband after his death, so a Christian is free from the law through his identification with Christ's death and resurrection. We are now married to Him in resurrection life.

The believer has also been quickened. The word *quickened* means "to be made alive." This correctly implies that a lost sinner is dead. Paul wrote, "And you hath he quickened, who were dead in trespasses and sins" (Eph 2:1; cf. 2:5). Paul added that men are also dead in the uncircumcision of their flesh (Col 2:13). A dead man cannot do anything for himself; his one need is life. Only God can make him spiritually alive. Just as God breathed into a lifeless body and Adam became a living soul, so God must breathe into the lifeless spirit of man. When God breathes, man responds. The believer has been just as permanently quickened from spiritual death as Christ has been made alive from the realm of physical death. Just as Christ can die no more, the believing sinner cannot either. He has a quickened position in the resurrected Christ (Eph 2:5-6).

The Christian is also a sanctified person. *Sanctify,* in its word derivation, means "to set apart." With reference to the child of God, it is used in three ways. First, at the moment of salvation, the believer was sanctified positionally. He was set apart from the world unto God. This is an accomplished fact and event. When Paul wrote to the Corinthian church, he addressed "them that are sanctified in Christ Jesus, called to be saints, with all that in every place call upon the name of Jesus Christ our Lord, both their's and our's" (1 Co 1:2). These carnal, sinning believers were nevertheless saints ("set apart ones"). Their position in Christ Jesus made possible their sanctification (1 Co 1:30; 6:11).

Second, there should be progressive sanctification taking place in the daily life of a Christian. God wants every believer to be holy as He is holy (1 Pe 1:16). This was part of Christ's concern in His intercessory prayer: "Sanctify them through thy truth: thy word is truth" (Jn 17:17). He also said, "And for their sakes I sanctify myself, that they also might be sanctified through the truth" (Jn 17:19). The believer's practice is not yet up to his position. He needs to be set apart daily from the influence of the sin nature, the system of the world, and the devil. Christ's death and resurrection, His ministry of intercession in the presence of God, and the application of the Word of God by the Holy Spirit can enable the believer to walk the holy, separated life.

Third, permanent sanctification will come at the return of Christ. Paul wrote:

> Husbands, love your wives, even as Christ also loved the church, and gave himself for it; That he might sanctify and cleanse it with the washing of water by the word, That he might present it to himself a glorious church, not having spot, or wrinkle, or any such thing; but that it should be holy and without blemish (Eph 5:25-27).

When will the believer be without moral spot or wrinkle? When will he be perfectly holy and without blemish? When the Christian sees Christ and is changed to be like Him (1 Jn 3:2), then he will be permanently set apart from the aftereffects and presence of sin.

The Christian has also been perfected. The author of Hebrews wrote, "For by one offering he hath perfected for ever them that are sanctified" (Heb 10:14). To perfect means to bring to completion, to the end, or to maturity or adulthood. Positionally, God sees us as perfected or completed persons. Christ offered one sacrifice for sins *forever*. (The same word is found in 10:12 and 14). His death was done in time; the results of it last forever. So it is with the act of divine perfection. It was done at conversion; its results continue into eternity. Positionally, the believer can be no more perfect than he is right now.

The Christian has been made meet. This is a strange, but scriptural, expression. In his prayer, Paul gave thanks to God the Father who "hath made us meet to be partakers of the inheritance of the saints in light" (Col 1:12). The believer has been rendered fit or sufficient by God to participate in the inheritance given to all saints. This is a work of God done in the believer's past at conversion. It is a completed work (note the verb tense) which produces an acceptable standing.

The best words to summarize the believer's relationship

to sin are *no condemnation*. Like the woman taken in adultery, the Christian is excited to hear these loving words from the Saviour, "Neither do I condemn thee: go, and sin no more" (Jn 8:11). Paul wrote, "There is therefore now no condemnation to them which are in Christ Jesus" (Ro 8:1). The guilt of sin, the penalty of sin, and the sins themselves have been erased. God could not condemn us any more than He could condemn His own Son, and we are in Him. Saving faith delivers from condemnation.

> He that believeth on him is not condemned: but he that believeth not is condemned already, because he hath not believed in the name of the only begotten Son of God (Jn 3:18).

Jesus also said that the believer would "not come into condemnation; but is passed from death unto life" (Jn 5:24). This is why a genuine Christian does not sense any moral guilt or the shadow of eternal wrath over him when an evangelistic message is being preached. He has peace with or before God by faith in Christ (Ro 5:1). God has instilled by the Spirit a sense of "no condemnation" within His child. There should be no fear within the Christian, but rather thanksgiving for what God has done for him and a prayerful concern for the lost. The Christian, of course, can sin; but he will never again experience the feeling of condemnation. Rather, he will experience shame for disobeying his Father. God will chastise His child for sin now; the sin of the world will be dealt with at the great white throne judgment (1 Co 11:32).

In this final section of chapter 2, we will deal with the titles and possessions that are ascribed to the Christian. The term *Christian* is actually used only three times in the New Testament (Ac 11:26; 26:28; 1 Pe 4:16). It was a title first given to believers by pagan Gentiles in Syrian Antioch. Herod Agrippa II was not persuaded by Paul to become one. Peter instructed his readers to suffer as Christians for the sake of righteousness. A Christian is a "Christone," one who is identified with Christ by belief and by behavior. Although this is the most popular designation used today, the Bible mentions many more varied titles for the believer.

A common description of believers is that they are the children of God. John wrote, "But as many as received him, to them gave he power to become the sons of God [children, Greek], even to them that believe on his name" (Jn 1:12). Men are not *born* children of God; they *become* children of God through saving faith in Christ. Just as natural children receive the nature of their parents, so the believing sinner receives the divine nature of his new Father.

A believer is also a son of God, as I mentioned earlier under the discussion of adoption. A person becomes a child of God by regeneration or the new birth; he is then adopted or put into the position of a full grown son by God. This gives him equal responsibilities and privileges with those Christians who have been saved longer (Gal 3:26–4:7). All believers have this position of sonship. To enjoy the everyday blessings of the Father-son relationship, one must live a holy, separated life (2 Co 6:17-18).

In Christ, the believer is a new creature. Paul stated, "Therefore if any man be in Christ, he is a new creature: old things are passed away; behold, all things are become new" (2 Co 5:17). This verse is commonly used to refer to the believer's habits. That is, if a person is genuinely saved, there will be a radical change in his behavior. The old habits of his past sinful life will be replaced by new patterns of holy behavior. However, this passage actually deals with a believer's position in Christ, not his practice. It is not true that all old bad habits are replaced by new

good ones. People bring into their daily Christian experience lots of bad attitudes, perspectives, and deeds.
This is why the New Testament is full of exhortations to
Christians to change their daily deportment. *But*, a person's position has completely changed. Note that the verb
tenses in this verse deal with the believer's past at the moment of salvation. He was once dead, but now he is alive (2
Co 5:14-15). He has been reconciled and made righteous (2
Co 5:18, 21). He was once in a lost, condemned position,
but now he is in a saved, acceptable position. The old
position has passed away; he now has a completely new
position before God. All believers share in the equality of
this new position: "For in Christ Jesus neither circumcision
availeth any thing nor uncircumcision, but a new creature"
(Gal 6:15). There is no advantage to the Jew or to the
Gentile. This created position will be evidenced practically
by the creation of good works in the life of the believer
(Eph 2:10).

Believers have been constituted by God as a holy and
royal priesthood (1 Pe 2:5, 9). This was made possible
through the redeeming, shed blood of Christ on the cross
(Rev 1:5-6; 5:9-10). We Christians will reign with Christ
on the earth during the millennial kingdom (Rev 5:10;
20:6). As priests, we are to offer spiritual sacrifices to God
today as well as in the future. What are these spiritual
sacrifices? They are the sacrifice of praise or giving thanks
(Heb 13:15-16), the sacrifice of financial giving (Phil
4:18), the sacrifice of self to live for Christ (Ro 12:1-2),
and for some, the sacrifice to die for Him (2 Ti 4:6). In the
patriarchal age, the senior male member of the family
functioned as the priest. After the exodus, the tribe of Levi
became the priestly class with the family of Aaron serving
as the high priestly family. Christ, by divine appointment,
became a high priest after the order of Melchisedec (Heb

5:5-6). This permitted Him to be both a king and a priest at the same time. Since we are in Christ, we share in His priesthood in the sense that we also serve as kings and priests forever before God. He has an unchangeable priesthood, and so do we (Heb 7:24).

The believer is part of a chosen generation (1 Pe 2:9). Christians are a new breed, a new race. They were chosen or elected in eternity past to be a member of this generation (Eph 1:4). Their nationality is not Jewish, Gentile, German, or Irish, but Christian. Just as a person never loses his genetic, racial traits, so a Christian can never lose his "chosen generation" identity.

He is also a member of an holy nation (1 Pe 2:9). He has been separated from the world unto God. *Holy* means "separated." His basic allegiance is to Christ's kingdom, which is not of this world (Jn 18:36).

Christians are a peculiar people, or, a people for God's exclusive possession (1 Pe 2:9). This was part of the goal of Christ's death: "Who [Christ] gave himself for us, that he might redeem us from all iniquity, and purify unto himself a peculiar people, zealous of good works" (Titus 2:14). Christians are not peculiar in a strange, odd fashion; rather, they are such because they belong to God. He has possessed us so that we might be pure and that we might be brought to Himself. This sets us apart as God's possession. Basically, we belong to Him rather than Him belonging to us.

The child of God is also recognized as an heavenly citizen. Although Paul was both a Jew and a Roman citizen, he declared, "For our conversation [citizenship, Greek] is in heaven; from whence also we look for the Saviour, the Lord Jesus Christ" (Phil 3:20). Every believer has his name written down in heaven (Lk 10:20). He is a member of the heavenly Jerusalem, a member of the "church of the firstborn, which are written in heaven" (Heb 12:22-23). He is a fellowcitizen with all other saints or believers (Eph 2:19). Like Abel, Noah, and Abraham, the Christians should confess to all that we are nothing but "strangers and pilgrims on the earth" (Heb 11:13). Every genuine Christian is marked by these words:

> For they that say such things declare plainly that they seek a country. And truly, if they had been mindful of that country from whence they came out, they might have had opportunity to have returned. But now they desire a better country, that is, an heavenly: wherefore God is not ashamed to be called their God: for he hath prepared for them a city (Heb 11:14-16).

A believer is essentially a tourist in this world. Peter's injunction to "abstain from fleshly lusts" is not based upon a possible loss of salvation as a threat, but rather upon the pilgrim character of the Christian (1 Pe 2:11).

Another relationship of the child of God is that he is a member of the household of God (Eph 2:19). Every believer is likened to a living stone or brick that is added to the spiritual house (1 Pe 2:5). The character of this building is thus described by Paul:

> And are built upon the foundation of the apostles and prophets, Jesus Christ himself being the chief corner stone; In whom all the building fitly framed together groweth unto an holy temple in the Lord: In whom ye also are builded together for an habitation of God through the Spirit (Eph 2:20-22).

Since he is in a living, vital relationship to other Christians as well as to God, the believer should "do good unto all men, especially unto them who are of the household of faith" (Gal 6:10). If a Christian could lose his salvation, then this would mean that a brick would be removed from

God's house. This would cause the collapse of other bricks, and the building would then be in a weakened, ugly condition. Would God be satisfied with this kind of house? Certainly not. The mortar that binds believers to one another is the ministry of the Holy Spirit, not the faithful deeds of the saints (Eph 2:22).

Every believer is an heir of God through Christ (Gal 4:7). He has "an inheritance incorruptible, and undefiled, and that fadeth not away, reserved in heaven" (1 Pe 1:4). Jesus said that this type of treasure could not be spoiled by moth, rust, or thief (Mt 6:19-20). An inheritance is not worked for; it is given freely by the testator. The value of the inheritance is based upon the wealth of the giver. A man can only give that which he himself possesses. These are the principles behind the giving of our *eternal* inheritance (Heb 9:15). Christ, eternal life personified, has willed or given eternal life to those who have been called according to divine purpose. This inheritance is guaranteed by the indwelling presence of the Holy Spirit and will be fully received at the coming of Jesus Christ.

The Christian is also a child of light. Christ is both life and light (Jn 1:4), and the believer shares in both of them. He is "light in the Lord" (Eph 5:8). As light, he is not destined to darkness, the darkness of the day of the Lord and the darkness of divine wrath (1 Th 5:4-9). Positionally, the child of God is morally and spiritually transparent in God's sight. There is not a single flaw or dark spot in his position. He is in the Lord Jesus, and Christ has no darkness.

If salvation were only a passport from hell to heaven, then it would be conceivable that a man could somehow lose or misplace it. But salvation is not something possessed by the hand; it is in the heart. In fact, it is more than a heart matter. It is an entire change of a person's position before God.

I have given a descriptive list of approximately fifty things that are true of every child of God. If a person could lose his salvation, every one of these positions would have to be reversed or forfeited, and the person would have to return to a totally guilty position before God. Salvation is not only *from* but also *to*. Loss of salvation would reverse it completely.

Remember, God has provided salvation, not just a chance or opportunity for salvation. He has given eternal life, not just temporary spiritual life that might eventually lead to everlasting life.

Some have looked upon salvation as a warranty contract, similar to a manufacturer's guarantee on the life of his product. At the bottom of the contract, in fine print, it states that the guarantee is only valid as long as there is no deliberate breakage, et cetera. That would be a good illustration if salvation were a product, but it is not. Salvation involves the total change of a person before God because he is now a new creation in Christ Jesus. Salvation is not purchased by the believing sinner; it is given by a gracious God.

Salvation is eternal. These positional, spiritual truths never change. "Blessed be the God and Father of our Lord Jesus Christ, who hath blessed us with all spiritual blessings in heavenly places in Christ" (Eph 1:3).

3

Does God Guarantee Our Salvation?

SALVATION MUST BE SEEN as a work of God. We are His workmanship, the work of His new creation (Eph 2:10). Salvation is basically theocentric, not anthropocentric. He has done the work, and He has done it for His eternal glory. Can any work of God be imperfect? Certainly not. The Creator has guaranteed the work of His hands and of His heart. It is beautiful and lasting.

According to the Scriptures, the promise of God guarantees our salvation. Jesus said, "He that heareth my word, and believeth on him that sent me, hath everlasting life, and shall not come into condemnation; but is passed from death unto life" (Jn 5:24). There are no ifs, ands, or buts. There is no fine print. There are no legal loopholes by which God can get out of His obligation. If a man believes, then that man *has* eternal life. He will *not* come into judgment; he is *already* passed from death to life. That verse is clear enough. Is God true to His Word and to what He promises? He certainly is. Jesus did not say that the person would have eternal life as long as he remained faithful, as long as he lived a life free from sin, et cetera. He has everlasting life—period!

The believer has the promise of no condemnation (Jn 3:16-18; Ro 8:1). He also has the promise of no separation. In answer to the question, "Who shall separate us from the love of Christ?" (Ro 8:35), Paul wrote these words:

71

> For I am persuaded, that neither death, nor life, nor
> angels, nor principalities, nor powers, nor things present,
> nor things to come, Nor height, nor depth, nor any other
> creature, shall be able to separate us from the love of
> God, which is in Christ Jesus our Lord (Ro 8:38-39).

In death, the soul separates from the body, but the believer
can never be separated from God. No angel, including
Satan, could ever sever the relationship between God and
His child. The deeds of tomorrow ("things to come") cannot break the bond either. Even the believer could not
separate himself. ("Any other creature" would certainly
include him.) What genuine believer would want to any-
way?

Some have suggested that a Christian could eventually
be separated from God but not from His love. But how
can you separate God's attributes from His person? Paul
had no fear of the future, because he saw no separation in
the future. All of us should live with God's Word ringing
in our ears and in our hearts: "I will never leave thee, nor
forsake thee" (Heb 13:5).

The believer's confidence rests not in what he thinks but
in what God has said. This is the argument of Hebrews
6:16-19:

> For men verily swear by the greater: and an oath for
> confirmation is to them an end of all strife. Wherein God,
> willing more abundantly to shew unto the heirs of prom-
> ise the immutability of his counsel, confirmed it by an
> oath: That by two immutable things, in which it was im-
> possible for God to lie, we might have a strong consola-
> tion, who have fled for refuge to lay hold upon the hope
> set before us: Which hope we have as an anchor of the
> soul, both sure and stedfast, and which entereth into that
> within the veil.

As Abraham's spiritual children, we are heirs according to

His promise (Gal 3:29). In fact, we have obtained an inheritance, "being predestinated according to the purpose of him who worketh all things after the counsel of his own will" (Eph 1:11). God does not lie. His oath and His promise are sure. They are immutable, unchanging. A believer could no more lose his salvation than Abraham could. God's promises to him were unconditional; they are the same to us. This truth should give to the believer comfort and stability, not unnecessary anxiety about the future.

The safekeeping of God also guarantees our salvation. No one could question the power or ability of God to keep the believing sinner. This is the testimony of Scripture: "Now unto him that is able to keep you from falling, and to present you faultless before the presence of his glory with exceeding joy" (Jude 24; cf. Ro 16:25). The issue is not with God's ability to keep but with His will to do so. Here, many Evangelicals part company. Does God *will* to keep His own? Arminians (those who believe that a Christian can lose his salvation) would reply in the affirmative but would refer the problem to God's permissive will. Just as God is not willing that any should perish (2 Pe 3:9), so He is not willing that any lose their salvation. However, God does not impose His will upon the unwilling person in either case, they say. On the other side of the theological issue, the Calvinists would argue that safekeeping is part of God's decretory or direct will. This type of will is always carried out. Which is it?

Peter wrote that believers "are kept by the power of God through faith unto salvation ready to be revealed in the last time" (1 Pe 1:5). Some would argue that God's power to keep is only as good as one's continuing faith. However, is Peter talking about daily faith in the life of a Christian or the initial act of faith which secures God's total gift of salvation? It is the latter. When a man receives Christ by faith, he becomes a saved person (Eph 2:8-9). God then keeps him until that time when he will also receive the salvation of his body (the immortal, incorruptible body).

Jude wrote to sanctified, preserved, and called Christians (Jude 1). This was a settled condition and fact. When were they sanctified and kept? At the time of their conversion, God did this for them, and they were now in this position or standing before God. (The verbs are in the Greek perfect tense). Their preservation was just as guaranteed as their justification and glorification (Ro 8:28-30), because all were included within God's direct will. These same three words are found in Paul's prayer for the Thessalonians:

> And the very God of peace sanctify you wholly; and I pray God your whole spirit and soul and body be preserved blameless unto the coming of our Lord Jesus Christ. Faithful is he that calleth you, who also will do it (1 Th 5:23-24).

Paul did not pray that the Thessalonians keep themselves; preservation is God's work. Paul knew this, and he also knew that God would do it because He is faithful to His Word.

Shortly before his martyrdom, Paul expressed this confidence: "And the Lord shall deliver me from every evil work, and will preserve me unto his heavenly kingdom" (2 Ti 4:18). Paul had no doubts about God's ability or His willingness or His direct purpose to do so. Earlier, in a most familiar verse, he testified, "I know whom I have believed, and am persuaded that he is able to keep that which I have committed unto him against that day" (2 Ti 1:12). There is a slight problem of translation and interpretation here. Paul was persuaded that God would guard what He had entrusted into Paul's care and charge, namely the ministry with its gifts. (See 1:14 where the same words are used for Timothy.) Actually, this is also an argument for preservation but from a different angle. If God can protect the ministry that He has committed to a Christian, He certainly can keep that person's salvation.

The safekeeping of the believer was one of the purposes in Christ's prayer of intercession. He prayed, "And now I am no more in the world, but these are in the world, and I come to thee. Holy Father, keep through thine own name those whom thou hast given me, that they may be one, as we are" (Jn 17:11). The principle of Scripture is that all prayer prayed in the will of God under the direction of the Holy Spirit will be answered. Did Jesus Christ, God the Son incarnate, ever pray *outside* the will of God? Certainly not! Therefore, His prayer must and will be answered. He also prayed, "I pray not that thou shouldest take them out of the world, but that thou shouldest keep them from the evil [one]" (Jn 17:15). The believer is to be kept in the world from the devil or Satan. If a Christian could lose his salvation, then the prayer of Christ would go unanswered. Think of the theological implications of that possibility. Was the Father impotent to keep? Was Jesus wrong in praying this way? Both questions require a negative answer. Safekeeping is partially God's response to Christ's prayer.

Probably the greatest safekeeping passage in Scripture is found in John 10:25-30:

> Jesus answered them, I told you, and ye believed not: the works that I do in my Father's name, they bear witness of me. But ye believe not, because ye are not of my sheep, as I said unto you. My sheep hear my voice, and I know them, and they follow me: And I give unto them eternal life; and they shall never perish, neither shall any man pluck them out of my hand. My Father, which gave

them me, is greater than all; and no man is able to pluck
them out of my Father's hand. I and my Father are one.

Jesus spoke this to the unbelieving Jews during the feast of
dedication. They did not believe *because* they were not
His sheep. Most would read it this way: "They were not
His sheep because they did not believe." But that is not
what it says. These are elected or called sheep, the gift of
the Father to the Son.

There are no conditions in this passage. He did not say,
"If they follow me, I will give them eternal life." These
are statements of absolute fact. There are five of them:

1. My sheep hear my voice.
2. I know them.
3. They follow me.
4. I give unto them eternal life.
5. They shall never perish.

The word *never* means *never*. In the Greek, it is extremely
emphatic.

The believer has double protection. He is in the hand of
the Son and also in the hand of the Father. The words
any one and *no one* are all inclusive. (*Man* is in italics;
these words refer both to human and angelic beings.) No
man can pluck us out. No angel, even Satan himself, can
pluck us out. God is holding us firmly in His grip; we are
not holding on to Him. However, some say that the believer can pluck himself out. How contrary to natural observation that statement is! Besides, is not the believer
himself included within the "anyone" and "no one" of the
verses? Now we can understand more fully Paul's statement, "Your life is hid with Christ in God" (Col 3:3).

As Christians, sheep of His fold, we are always under
the care of the Shepherd, Jesus Christ (Jn 10:1-16). True,
it is our nature to wander: "Prone to wander, Lord, I feel

it, Prone to leave the God I love." *But,* it is His nature to keep us, to seek us out, and to bring us back into His fold. Remember the shepherd who left the fold to retrieve the lost, erring sheep (Lk 15:3-7)? With David, we can praise and sing:

> The LORD is my shepherd; I shall not want.
>
> He maketh me to lie down in green pastures: he leadeth me beside the still waters.
>
> He restoreth my soul: he leadeth me in the paths of righteousness for his name's sake.
>
> Yea, though I walk through the valley of the shadow of death, I will fear no evil: for thou art with me; thy rod and thy staff they comfort me.
>
> Thou preparest a table before me in the presence of mine enemies: thou anointest my head with oil; my cup runneth over.
>
> Surely goodness and mercy shall follow me all the days of my life: and I will dwell in the house of the LORD for ever (Ps 23).

The grace of God also guarantees our salvation. How familiar Paul's words are: "For by grace are ye saved through faith; and that not of yourselves: it is the gift of God: Not of works, lest any man should boast" (Eph 2:8-9). The entire program of salvation is immersed in divine grace. Salvation is saturated with grace from the beginning to the end. The believing sinner has been saved by grace and stands as a saved person by grace before a holy God. (The words *are saved* from the Greek mean that a person has entered into a saved position and permanently stays in that condition; cf. Ro 5:1-2.) Man's works could never give him salvation nor guarantee that salvation. A man is both saved and kept by divine grace. Paul wrote: "Therefore it is of faith, that it might be by grace; to the end the promise might be sure to all the seed"

(Ro 4:16). The future unfaithfulness of Abraham did not negate the fulfillment of the promise. A grace program depends solely upon God for its completion.

The concept of grace is greatly misunderstood these days. Some have defined *grace* as "*God's riches at Christ's expense.*" Man does not work for grace; it is given to him. Man cannot pay it back either. Grace is when God chooses to give man favor, out of His divine graciousness apart from any merit in man, either past, present, or future. Jesus taught,

> For if ye love them which love you, what thank have ye? for sinners also love those that love them. And if ye do good to them which do good to you, what thank have ye? for sinners also do even the same. And if ye lend to them of whom ye hope to receive, what thank have ye, for sinners also lend to sinners, to receive as much again. But love ye your enemies, and do good, and lend, hoping for nothing again; and your reward shall be great, and ye shall be the children of the Highest: for he is kind unto the unthankful and to the evil (Lk 6:32-35).

Substitute "grace" for "thank" (grace, Greek), and read that passage again. Grace gives without expecting anything in return. No man could do anything before God to deserve His grace, and no man after receiving saving grace could ever expect to do enough to justify the keeping of that grace. He is saved and sustained by grace. The doctrine of eternal security definitely harmonizes with the doctrine of grace far more than the position that salvation can be lost through sin or lack of faith.

As a recipient of God's saving grace, the believer is in a far more advantageous position to receive the sustaining grace of God, "grace for grace" (Jn 1:16). Listen to Paul:

> For when we were yet without strength, in due time Christ died for the ungodly. For scarcely for a righteous

man will one die: yet peradventure for a good man some would even dare to die. But God commendeth his love toward us, in that, while we were yet sinners, Christ died for us. Much more then, being now justified by his blood, we shall be saved from wrath through him. For if, when we were enemies, we were reconciled to God by the death of his Son, much more, being reconciled, we shall be saved by his life (Ro 5:6-10).

If God did so much for us when we were without strength, ungodly, sinners, and enemies, imagine what He will do for us now that we are His children! *Much more!* Humanly speaking, getting us saved was the hard job; keeping us saved is easy in comparison. Safekeeping is the gift wrapping around the gift of salvation. This is what Paul meant in Romans 8:32: "He that spared not his own Son, but delivered him up for us all, how shall he not with him also freely give us all things?"

Under grace: nothing can be added or subtracted from that glorious position. Paul wrote: "For sin shall not have dominion over you: for ye are not under the law, but under grace" (Ro 6:14). No sin can remove the believer from that spiritual standing. Sin does not stop the flow of divine grace or remove the past gifts of grace; in fact, it is sin that stimulates grace. It is because of sin that grace is manifested. "But where sin abounded, grace did much more abound" (Ro 5:20). If sin could cost a believer his salvation, then that sin would have a greater power than grace. Impossible! Just as grace can save the worst and chief of sinners, so it can overcome the worst sin that a Christian could commit. Divine grace does much more than man could ever expect or think.

The unconditional purposes of God further guarantee the salvation of the believer. Whatever God decrees or wills to do will be done. In our time-and-space universe, from the human standpoint, it takes time to accomplish the purpose of God. However, from God's eternal viewpoint, the purposes of His will are regarded as established facts. This is why the child of God can be optimistic and realistic about his life: "And we know that all things work together for good to them that love God, to them who are the called according to his purpose" (Ro 8:28). He knows that he is the object of God's purpose which includes foreknowledge, predestination, calling, justification, and glorification. If a person is really a called one according to divine purpose, then he will definitely experience glorification. There can be no doubt about that. Look at your own life. Do you not think that God knew about your postconversion sins and unfaithfulness in eternity past? Certainly He did, and in spite of that, He decreed your justification and glorification. God completes what He has determined to do. The sin of man does not take God by surprise, nor does it prevent the fulfillment of His purpose.

God's purposes are "according to the good pleasure of his will" (Eph 1:5). They are not based upon man's good works, either before or after salvation. How could any man *will* to be lost? Is man's will greater than God's will? To ask the question is to answer it. Nothing can circumvent the pleasure of God's will.

The ultimate purpose behind salvation is "that in the ages to come he might shew the exceeding riches of his grace in his kindness toward us through Christ Jesus" (Eph 2:7). If a Christian possessed and lost the riches of divine grace, God, in eternity future, could say, "I gave him what he deserved." But, how would that magnify His grace? Grace gives to undeserving sinners. Which one of us could ever say that he deserves eternal heaven for five, ten, or twenty years of faithful Christian living? We must all admit with Paul, "But by the grace of God I am what I am" (1 Co 15:10).

The purposes of God include security goals. He will confirm every believer to the end (1 Co 1:8). Believers, both spiritual (Paul) and carnal (Corinthian Christians), will bear the image of the heavenly one, receiving the new immortal body (1 Co 15:49, 53). God is bringing many sons into glory (Heb 2:10). The believer can have total confidence that God who has "begun a good work in [him] will perform it until the day of Jesus Christ" (Phil 1:6). In practical application, the Christian must work out what God is working within him "both to will and to do of [God's] good pleasure" (Phil 2:12-13). God's will to mold and to keep finds expression through man's desire to live for Him and to serve Him. If a man is not working out his salvation position, then it may mean that God is not working in him. He may not have genuine salvation to begin with. He may not be one of the called according to divine purpose.

God's choice of Jacob rather than Esau rested upon the purpose of His will, not theirs. Some would call this unfair, but these people simply do not understand the holy, pure character of God or the total sinfulness of man (Ro 9:14, 19-21). If the manifestation of divine mercy and grace depended upon the goodness of man, then it would never be given. Paul wrote, "So then it is not of him that willeth, nor of him that runneth, but of God that showeth mercy" (Ro 9:16). God will have mercy and compassion upon whom He wills to have mercy. God has a perfect right to do what He pleases. If God wills to manifest mercy to a sinner who after salvation leads a carnal, backsliding life, then God can do it. We should be amazed at God's mercy and grace, and we should be thankful for it. God wants to "make known the riches of his glory on the vessels of mercy, which he had afore prepared unto glory" (Ro 9:23).

The intercession ministry of Jesus Christ, both past and present, also guarantees our salvation. When He walked upon this earth, He prayed not only for the apostles but for all future believers (Jn 17:9; cf. 17:20). He did not pray for the lost world (17:9); that is our responsibility. For what did He pray? He prayed that we might be kept by the Father from the evil one (17:11, 15). He prayed that we might have His joy fulfilled in us (17:13). He prayed for our sanctification through the word of truth (17:17). He prayed for our spiritual unity (17:21). He prayed that we might be made perfect in one (17:23). He prayed that we might be with Him in heaven (17:24). He prayed that we might behold His glory (17:24). He prayed that the same love that the Father has for the Son might be in us (17:26). What a prayer! Again, here is the scriptural principle of prayer: all prayer prayed in the will of God by the Holy Spirit will be answered by God. Was this prayer expressed in the will of God? Yes, completely, from the beginning to the end. It, therefore, will be answered totally.

Christ is not idle in heaven today. Although He finished the work of redemption through His death and resurrection, He continues His work of prayer in our behalf. Paul said that He is at the right hand of God, making intercession for us (Ro 8:34). It is no accident that His work of intercession is inserted between the "no condemnation" and "no separation" sections of this scripture passage. Christ's resurrection life has given Him an unchangeable priesthood (Heb 7:24). Because of this fact, He "is able also to save them to the uttermost that come unto God by him, seeing he ever liveth to make intercession for them" (Heb 7:25). Salvation, complete in all of its parts (what the word *uttermost* means), is made possible through

Christ's resurrection and His present ministry of prayer in our behalf. He is now appearing in the presence of God for us (Heb 9:24). Salvation is based upon His three appearings: first, at Calvary to put away sin by the sacrifice of Himself (Heb 9:26); second, today in heaven to pray for us and to represent us; and third, at His coming to receive us (Heb 9:28).

He is not only our intercessor but also our advocate. John wrote, "My little children, these things write I unto you, that ye sin not. And if any man sin, we have an advocate with the Father, Jesus Christ the righteous" (1 Jn 2:1). An advocate is one who has been called to stand beside you. He is like a lawyer. When a believer sins, Christ takes up His position beside that believer before God. He points out that His death on Calvary's cross took care of all sins, both before and after regeneration. The advocacy of Christ always guarantees the believer that he will never suffer eternal wrath for his sin, because Christ has already borne that penalty. One self-appointed task of Satan is that he accuses the brethren before God day and night (Rev 12:10). He points his finger at the sinning believer, demanding his eternal condemnation. But, the wonderful truth is that God sees us in His Son, and Satan cannot point his finger at Christ.

The night before His crucifixion, Jesus alarmed Peter by saying to him,

> Simon, Simon, behold, Satan hath desired to have you, that he may sift you as wheat: But I have prayed for thee, that thy faith fail not: and when thou art converted, strengthen thy brethren (Lk 22:31-32).

Satan asked God for permission to test Simon Peter just as he had tested Job. It was granted, and in the next few hours, Peter would know the agony of denial three times. However, in the midst of this trial, his faith would stand, supported by the answered prayer of Christ. Job learned patience and the folly of self-righteousness through his trial. Peter needed to have his pride and cockiness changed to humility and dependence upon God. How many times has Satan asked to test you, and how many times has Christ prayed that your faith fail not? Who knows, but God?

The salvation of the believer is also guaranteed by the obedience of Jesus Christ to the will of God.

> All that the Father giveth me shall come to me; and him that cometh to me I will in no wise cast out. For I came down from heaven, not to do mine own will, but the will of him that sent me. And this is the Father's will which hath sent me, that of all which he hath given me I should lose nothing, but should raise it up again at the last day. And this is the will of him that sent me, that every one which seeth the Son, and believeth on him, may have everlasting life: and I will raise him up at the last day (Jn 6:37-40).

No one can question the fact that Christ came into the world to do the will of God, that He did it, and that He is doing it now. Since every believer is a gift from the Father to the Son, every one of these will come to Christ. No believer will ever, for any reason, be cast out nor lost by Him. He will give that believing sinner both everlasting and resurrection life. If one Christian could lose his salvation, then Christ would be disobeying the will of God. Salvation is not a question of a person losing it, but a question of Christ keeping or losing those whom the Father has given to Him. This is why Christ later said that no one could ever pluck the believer out of His Hand (Jn 10:28). Holding the believer firm in the divine clasp is part of His obedience.

The purpose of Christ's redemptive work also guarantees

our salvation. In his instructions to Christian husbands, Paul exhorted,

> Husbands, love your wives, even as Christ also loved the church, and gave himself for it; That he might sanctify and cleanse it with the washing of water by the word, That he might present it to himself a glorious church, not having spot, or wrinkle, or any such thing; but that it should be holy and without blemish (Eph 5:25-27).

If all believers, members of the true church, were not presented eventually to Him, then the church indeed would be marred. It would be spotted, wrinkled, or blemished. Christ has made every provision for a total presentation of all believers in holiness. His love, sacrifice, sanctification, and cleansing guarantee this future presentation.

Christ became "the author of eternal salvation" through His obedience on the cross (Heb 5:9). What does "eternal" mean? He did not become the author of contingent salvation, of temporary salvation, of a chance for salvation. He became the author of *eternal* salvation. If salvation is not eternal, it is not salvation.

Peter wrote, "For Christ also hath once suffered for sins, the just for the unjust, that he might bring us to God" (1 Pe 3:18). We do not take ourselves to God; *He* brings us to God. The loss of salvation would reflect upon His "bringing" power. If all who have believed are not brought, then the purpose of His vicarious sufferings has been thwarted.

The abiding presence of the Holy Spirit also guarantees our salvation. In the preceding chapter, the believer's relationship to the Holy Spirit was described. He has been regenerated, sealed, and baptized with the Spirit. The Spirit is God's earnest to us. We do not give Him a pledge of our faith which we can withdraw at any moment.

Rather, God gives us the Holy Spirit as His pledge that we will receive all that He has purposed and promised. All of these blessings are directly related to the indwelling presence of the Spirit in the believer's life. Jesus said:

> And I will pray the Father, and he shall give you another Comforter, that he may abide with you for ever; Even the Spirit of truth; whom the world cannot receive, because it seeth him not, neither knoweth him: but ye know him; for he dwelleth with you, and shall be in you (Jn 14:16-17).

The Spirit is eternally in the life of the believer in response to Christ's prayer to the Father. There are no conditions in this passage. He abides with us and in us forever.

God has definitely guaranteed our salvation. It cannot be lost.

4

Do You Know These Scriptural Principles?

To some Christians, verse memorization and quotation is the epitome and substance of scriptural knowledge. If you ask them a question, they reply with a quoted Bible verse and nothing more. If you ask them what that verse means or how it relates to a passage in another book, many times they are unable to answer. All of us should hide God's Word in our hearts (Ps 119:11), but that is just the point. To hide God's Word and to memorize Bible verses may not always be the same thing. Do you know what the verse means? How does it fit into the paragraph or passage? How can it be correlated with other passages and verses into a systematic presentation of doctrine? Can you perceive the divine principles that run throughout His Word? When you are aware and sensitive to all of these areas, then memorize the scripture verse; it will mean more then.

This is also true in the study of eternal security. Undergirding key verses are great principles that must be recognized. They reflect one's "sense" of Scripture, a grasp of the general tenor of the Bible. They form the background against which individual verses can be studied. Let us look at these principles now.

First, initial salvation is not repeatable. There was a true, observable principle behind the question of Nicodemus: "How can a man be born when he is old? can he enter the second time into his mother's womb, and be born?" (Jn 3:4). Naturally, he cannot; once you are born, you are always born. That action cannot be reversed or repeated. So it is with the divine birth. It would be impossible for a man, saved twenty or thirty years, to crawl back into the divine womb and be born spiritually all over again.

The brazen serpent experience of Israel in the wilderness illustrates Calvary and salvation. John wrote, "And as Moses lifted up the serpent in the wilderness, even so must the Son of man be lifted up: That whosoever believeth in him should not perish, but have eternal life" (Jn 3:14-15). God had punished Israel for their murmuring by sending poisonous snakes into their midst. People were bitten and died. In desperation, they had cried out to God in repentance, confessing their sins. God had instructed Moses, "Make thee a fiery serpent, and set it upon a pole: and it shall come to pass, that every one that is bitten, when he looketh upon it, shall live" (Num 21:8). How many times did the people have to look at the serpent to be healed? Just once. One look prompted by faith was enough. So it is with Calvary. How many times must one look at Christ in faith to be saved? Just once. The faith that heals or saves is an act, a completed event, not an attitude. In Bunyan's classic, *Pilgrim's Progress,* Pilgrim took one look at the uplifted Saviour, and his load of sin fell off his back forever.

When Jesus was dealing with the adulterous Samaritan woman at the well of Sychar, He spoke of both natural and spiritual thirst: "Whosoever drinketh of this water shall thirst again: But whosoever drinketh of the water that I shall give him shall never thirst; but the water that I shall give him shall be in him a well of water springing up into everlasting life" (Jn 4:13-14). The verb *drinketh* occurs twice in this passage. It is used in the Greek present tense to indicate physical drinking; man must drink over and over again of natural water to sustain physical life. However, the verb is used in the aorist tense in describing the spiritual drink. He just has to have one spiritual drink of Christ and he will have spiritual life. There is also a contrast in the thirsts. Men are always thirsty for natural water, but Jesus said that *one* spiritual drink will forever quench man's spiritual thirst. The Greek text is far more forceful: "He shall not, he shall not thirst forever." He shall absolutely not thirst again, either in this age or in eternity (double negative in the Greek text). If a Christian could lose his salvation and later gain it back, that would mean that he would have to drink and have to be thirsty all over again. Jesus called that an impossible situation. The believer's soul can thirst daily for God as the deer pants for the water brooks (Ps 42:1-2), but this is a different thirst. Thirst for salvation is forever satisfied by receiving Christ; thirst for fellowship should be a daily drive in the life of the Christian.

The contrast between the natural and the spiritual is also seen in the sermon on the bread of life. The five thousand shared in the multiplication of the five loaves of bread and the two fish, but the next day, they were hungry again. Jesus challenged them, "Labour not for the meat which perisheth, but for that meat which endureth unto everlasting life, which the Son of man shall give unto you" (Jn 6:27). How often children can get up from the lunch table and ask, "What are we going to have for supper?" One hour after supper, they are back in the kitchen getting their evening snacks. But, how differently is spiritual hunger satisfied! Jesus said, "I am the bread of life: he that cometh to me shall never hunger; and he that believeth on me shall never thirst" (Jn 6:35). Here, He combined

spiritual hunger with spiritual thirst. By coming and believing, they are forever satisfied. When a person receives
Christ as Saviour, the emptiness of his soul is forever filled
with the divine presence. He will never hunger for Christ
in this way again. True, he must drink of the milk and eat
of the meat of the Word of God to grow spiritually, but
the initial saving act of eating is past and complete. Jesus
added, "I am the living bread which came down from
heaven: if any man eat [again, aorist tense] of this bread,
he shall live for ever" (Jn 6:51). One act of eating gives
eternal life.

Think how the teaching of the Mass has distorted this
beautiful concept. Catholics believe that they receive
Christ in the transubstantiated wafer and wine. If they
could, why must they repeat the act daily or weekly? Why
are they not forever satisfied? Why do they continue to
hunger and to thirst spiritually? Christ is not received in
a wafer; He is received by the heart and will once for all
(Jn 1:12). When He is, the hunger and the thirst of the
lost sinner are quenched.

In the Garden of Eden, God commanded Adam, "But of
the tree of the knowledge of good and evil, thou shalt not
eat of it: for in the day that thou eatest thereof thou shalt
surely die" (Gen 2:17). How many times did Adam have
to eat to bring condemnation upon himself and the human race? Only once! One eating brought death. So it is
with salvation; one eating brings eternal life.

A second principle is that genuine, saving faith will produce genuine works of righteousness in the life. Jesus said,
"Even so every good tree bringeth forth good fruit; but a
corrupt tree bringeth forth evil fruit. A good tree cannot
bring forth evil fruit, neither can a corrupt tree bring forth
good fruit" (Mt 7:17-18). Inner nature is manifested by
the outward expression of that nature, namely, its fruit:

"Wherefore by their fruits ye shall know them" (Mt 7:20). Since no man, in his own nature, can do good (Ro 3:12), then good fruit or works of righteousness must be evidence that the divine nature dwells within him.

Jesus taught, "If ye continue in my word, then are ye my disciples indeed; And ye shall know the truth, and the truth shall make you free" (Jn 8:31-32). He said that to Jews who had "believed" on Him. Was it a genuine or a false faith? Was it only intellectual persuasion, or was it a real heart and will commitment to Christ? Time would tell. Would they continue in His Word? If they would, then this would be the evidence that they were genuine disciples. If they would not continue, then this would be the sign that they were not actually saved in the first place.

In His sermon on the good Shepherd, Jesus remarked, "My sheep hear my voice, and I know them, and they follow me" (Jn 10:27; cf. 10:4-5). The mark of His sheep is that they follow Him. If there is no following, this may be the evidence that the person may not be a genuine sheep of His fold, a real believer.

The grace of God that saved the sinner also teaches him about the essence of the Christian life. If a person is a genuine child of God, there will be evidence of the denial of ungodliness and wordly lusts and of the practice of the sober, righteous, godly life (Titus 2:11-12). The purpose of redemption is to produce a people "zealous of good works" (Titus 2:14). When a person genuinely perceives and receives the personification of grace and love of Calvary, he goes away with a determination to live for Christ. If this is lacking, the salvation experience can be questioned. Many Cretian "Christians" professed that they knew God, but in their works, they denied Him (Titus 1:16).

Contrary to the thinking of many, there is no contradic-

tion between Paul and James. Paul wrote that "a man is
justified by faith without the deeds of the law" (Ro 3:28),
and James wrote, "Ye see then how that by works a man
is justified, and not by faith only" (Ja 2:24). On the sur-
face, it may appear to be a doctrinal contradiction, but
upon closer investigation, a beautiful harmony emerges.
James argued, "What doth it profit, my brethren, though a
man say he hath faith, and have not works? can faith save
him?" (Ja 2:14). The important word is *say*. James con-
trasts the faith of lip profession with the faith of life expression. If a man *says* that he has faith, but there is no
evidence of that faith in life, can that type of faith save
him? Certainly not! The demons believe in God, in eternal
punishment, in creation, et cetera. They could probably
sign an orthodox doctrinal statement, but does that make
them saved? No! Why? Because it has never issued in a
transformation of life. Abraham manifested his faith by
offering Isaac. Rahab manifested her faith by hiding the
Jewish spies. The principle is: "Seest thou how faith
wrought with his works, and by works was faith made
perfect?" (Ja 2:22). John Calvin, the great reformer, said
that faith alone in Christ saved, but the faith that saved
is not alone. A man is not saved by faith *and* works; he is
saved by faith *that* works. Works are the breath of faith
(Ja 2:26). If you came upon an auto accident and found
a body lying still on the pavement, how could you tell
whether the person was dead or merely unconscious? Put
a mirror by his nose. If the mirror fogs up, he is still alive.
Is the faith of the lip a living faith or a dead faith? Works
of faith upon the mirror of experience give evidence of
genuine spiritual life. Paul, likewise, contended that a
saved person had been "created in Christ Jesus unto good
works, which God hath before ordained that we should

walk in them" (Eph 2:10). A living, genuine faith will produce works of faith.

This is why Peter admonished his readers, "Give diligence to make your calling and election sure" (2 Pe 1:10). How can a person be sure that he is one of the elect of God? Peter said, "And beside this, giving all diligence, add to your faith—" (2 Pe 1:5). What should be added? Add virtue, knowledge, temperance, patience, godliness, brotherly kindness, and love. If the fruit of the Christian life is being grown, there will be no doubt that the life of Christ, the divine nature, resides within.

Third, doctrinal consistency is a test of whether genuine salvation exists. Proper doctrine is essential to salvation. A person must believe in these doctrines in order to become a Christian: the existence of God, the sinfulness of man, the deity of Jesus Christ, the substitutionary death and bodily resurrection of Christ, and the necessity of the regeneration of the Holy Spirit. He must not only be intellectually and morally convinced of these truths but must willingly receive the person of Christ into his life. A genuine, initial belief and reception will continue throughout the person's life. The genuine Christian will never waver from this doctrinal position, or deny it.

In his warning to the elect lady, John cautioned, "Whosoever transgresseth, and abideth not in the doctrine of Christ, hath not God. He that abideth in the doctrine of Christ, he hath both the Father and the Son" (2 Jn 9). Abiding in the doctrine is evidence that one has God. Abiding not in the doctrine is proof that one has not God. A person does not move into and out of doctrinal orthodoxy. He is either in or out.

Paul also warned in this direction. He told the Colossians that God would "present you holy and unblameable

and unreproveable in his sight: If ye continue in the faith
grounded and settled, and be not moved away from the
hope of the gospel" (Col 1:22-23). As you can see, the
problem is with the conditional clause, "if ye continue in
the faith." There will be no presentation if there is no con-
tinuance. Practicing doctrinal orthodoxy guarantees the
ultimate presentation. The threat at Colosse came from
Judaistic Gnosticism, a merger of Greek philosophy with
Jewish legalism within a framework of false Christian doctrine. This heresy denied that Jesus Christ had two na-
tures, human and divine. It denied the incarnation, that
Christ had become man. It taught that matter was in-
nately evil; therefore, God, pure spirit, could never have
created this material universe directly. It taught the worship of angels as intermediaries between God and man.
Paul warned that acceptance of this heresy would guarantee no future presentation before God. If a person could
succumb to this intellectual heresy, it would be evidence
that he never really understood the doctrinal implications
of the gospel. He had given creedal assent to a "philosophy" that had sounded good to his ears, but he had never
fully embraced and appropriated the blood of Christ's cross
(Col 1:20). The "faith and hope" of this passage refer to
firm doctrinal convictions, not to some personal sins.

Fourth, genuine works produced by a believer will always be rewarded by God. The Bible speaks of rewards or
crowns that can be gained by the child of God for faithful
Christian service and living. The incorruptible crown will
be given to those who live the disciplined life under the
dual control of the Holy Spirit and self (1 Co 9:25). The
crown of rejoicing will be awarded those who have been
faithful and effective in witnessing for Christ (1 Th 2:19).
The crown of righteousness will be given to those who have
fulfilled God's will for their lives and who love the coming

of Christ (2 Ti 4:7-8). The crown of life will be received by those who have endured trials joyfully (Ja 1:12). The crown of glory will be given to pastors who have faithfully guided the work of local churches (1 Pe 5:4). Naturally, if a person could lose his salvation, he would also lose the rewards of those true, faithful postconversion experiences. But the Bible teaches that God will remember and reward each righteous work produced by the Spirit in the believer's life.

As an encouragement to the Hebrew Christians to go on with God to spiritual maturity, the author wrote, "For God is not unrighteous to forget your work and labour of love, which ye have shewed toward his name, in that ye have ministered to the saints, and do minister" (Heb 6:10). If God failed to reward Christian love and work, He would be unrighteous. He would not be giving men the reward or "bonus" He promised them. Employers may cheat their employees, causing a strike or a series of negotiations, but God will faithfully "pay" men for their Christian service.

Paul said, "Therefore, my beloved brethren, be ye stedfast, unmoveable, always abounding in the work of the Lord, for as much as ye know that your labour is not in vain in the Lord" (1 Co 15:58). If there were no resurrection of the dead, Paul argued, then labor would be for nought. If labor would go unrewarded, then it also would be in vain. In the days of Nehemiah, some Israelites complained about the value of their service, especially when the wicked were prospering around them. They cried, "It is vain to serve God: and what profit is it that we have kept his ordinance" (Mal 3:14). The answer came back quickly. Malachi wrote, "Then they that feared the LORD spake often one to another: and the LORD hearkened, and heard it, and a book of remembrance was written before him for them that feared the LORD, and that thought upon his name" (Mal 3:16).

God has a book of remembrance. He will not forget what men have done for Him. In His time and in His way, He will reward. Never believe that your work is useless or that it goes unnoticed. Jesus said that what is done in secret will be rewarded openly (Mt 5:4, 6, 18).

Every Christian will be praised at the judgment seat of Christ, which occurs just after Christ returns to take Christians into heaven (1 Co 4:5). Paul gave this description of that event:

> For other foundation can no man lay than that is laid, which is Jesus Christ. Now if any man build upon this foundation gold, silver, precious stones, wood, hay, stubble; Every man's work shall be made manifest: for the day shall declare it, because it shall be revealed by fire; and the fire shall try every man's work of what sort it is. If any man's work abide which he hath built thereupon, he shall receive a reward. If any man's work shall be burned, he shall suffer loss: but he himself shall be saved; yet so as by fire (1 Co 3:11-15).

Rewards are given for quality work and life-character built upon the saving foundation of Christ. Valueless works will be burned up, and the person will suffer the loss of reward. The person's life is still saved, however, because the foundation cannot be destroyed. Since all men will be praised in that day (1 Co 4:5), God will find something good to say about the Christian whose works are destroyed. This means that even the slightest work of righteousness will be remembered and rewarded. If a person is a genuine Christian, this means that at some periods in his life, he did that which was right before God. The major part of his life may be wasted, but those minor, blessed days will not go unnoticed. He will be saved, yet so as by fire, but he will still be saved.

Here is the fifth principle. In the epistles, the exhortations to live the godly life are based upon what God has done and plans to do in the Christian's life, not on the fear of losing one's salvation. Go through the writings of Paul and you will sense this principle. How easy it would have been for him to write, "Do this, or else you will end up in hell." But, he never does. Instead, he wrote like this:

> I beseech you therefore, brethren, by the mercies of God, that ye present your bodies a living sacrifice, holy, acceptable unto God, which is your reasonable service. And be not conformed to this world: but be ye transformed by the renewing of your mind, that ye may prove what is that good, and acceptable, and perfect, will of God (Ro 12:1-2).

In the following chapters, Paul talked about the believer's responsibilities within the church, in a pagan society, and to fellow Christians in nonmoral issues. These could only be fulfilled by a person who has completely yielded himself to the Lordship of Christ and to the will of God, by a person who fully appreciates and loves the mercies of God. What are the mercies of God? In the first eight chapters of Romans, Paul described God's magnificent plan for the Christian, including his justification, sanctification, and glorification (total salvation). Because of what God has done (justification), what God is doing (sanctification), and what God will yet do for you (glorification), present yourselves!

Paul said that the love of Christ constrained him to serve Him. He reasoned, "And that [Christ] died for all, that they which live should not henceforth live unto themselves, but unto him which died for them, and rose again" (2 Co 5:15). Paul's motivation to live for Christ came from the cross. If Christ loved him so much to die for him, how could Paul do other than live for Him? Should we

not do the same? Which is the higher and more scriptural
motivation: to live for Him out of love for what He has
done for you, or to live for Him out of fear that you might
lose your salvation if you do not? The one is a Christ-
centered life; the other is a self-centered and a self-moti-
vated life.

The argument of Ephesians is the same. After describing the wealth of spiritual possessions the believer has in
Christ, Paul admonished, "I therefore, the prisoner of the
Lord, beseech you that ye walk worthy of the vocation
wherewith ye are called" (Eph 4:1). Note that Paul said
"beseech" rather than "command." Later, he told the
Ephesian converts not to lie, not to steal, not to speak dirty.
He wrote, "But fornication, and all uncleanness, or covet-
ousness, let it not be once named among you, as becometh
saints" (Eph 5:3). Such terrible sins could be committed
by the Christian who still has a sin nature within himself.
The appeal not to practice them, however, is not based
upon a threat of possible loss of salvation, but rather upon
a proper understanding as to who Christians really are.
They *are* saints; therefore, they should not sin.

The sixth principle is that sin committed by the Christian severs fellowship with the heavenly Father, but not
relationship. God is light, or, morally transparent; He is
holiness personified. There is not a single speck of moral
flaw in His character (1 Jn 1:5). If a Christian is walking
in sin, he cannot possibly be having fellowship with Him
(1 Jn 1:6). Light and darkness cannot exist together;
therefore a holy God and an unholy person can not have
communion. True fellowship *is* possible for the Christian,
however. John wrote, "But if we walk in the light, as he
is in the light, we have fellowship one with another, and
the blood of Jesus Christ his Son cleanseth us from all sin"
(1 Jn 1:7).

The sense of fellowship, however, can be broken by sinful acts and attitudes. How can the fellowship be restored? Not by a new regeneration but by an honest confession: "If we confess our sins, he is faithful and just to forgive us our sins, and to cleanse us from all unrighteousness" (1 Jn 1:9). The Father-son relationship is not broken by sin; only the sweet fellowship is lost by the believer. This is what the prodigal son had to learn. After wasting his riches and his life, he decided to return home. When he arrived, he said, "Father, I have sinned against heaven, and in thy sight, and am no more worthy to be called thy son" (Lk 15:21). He underestimated the love and understanding of his father. Did the father grant his request? No! Rather, he said,

> Bring forth the best robe, and put it on him; and put a ring on his hand, and shoes on his feet: And bring hither the fatted calf, and kill it; and let us eat, and be merry: For this my son was dead, and is alive again; he was lost, and is found. And they began to be merry (Lk 15:22-24).

The son felt that the father-son relationship should be dissolved because of his actions, but fathers do not think that way. There was no criticism by the father. He did not give his son a lecture nor beat him. Rather, he opened his arms, his heart, and his house to the blessings of renewed fellowship. So it is with God. We may think that the Father-son relationship is over because of personal sin. We probably deserve the loss of salvation, but God does not operate the way we do. God said to erring Israel,

> Let the wicked forsake his way, and the unrighteous man his thoughts: and let him return unto the LORD, and he will have mercy upon him; and to our God, for he will abundantly pardon. For my thoughts are not your

thoughts, neither are your ways my ways, saith the LORD (Is 55:7-8).

Mercy and pardon await the returning child, not judgment. If man were given the place of God, he would probably condemn for the least sin, but man is not God. He lacks the character of God, especially His grace; therefore, he does not completely understand God's treatment of repentant believers. This was Jonah's problem. He was angry over the deliverance of Nineveh; he preferred its destruction. He knew that God was "a gracious God, and merciful, slow to anger, and of great kindness" (Jon 4:2). He wanted to give Nineveh what it deserved; God was willing to withhold what they deserved and to give them what they did not deserve.

At the washing of the disciples' feet, Jesus said to Peter, "If I wash thee not, thou hast no part with me" (Jn 13:8). Communion between the Saviour and His own does not require repeated baths of regeneration (Jn 13:10), only daily washings of the soul that has become soiled walking through a hostile world. The debates of the disciples about greatness and the future boastings that led to denials were not erased by a "new" new birth, but by confession and repentance.

Seventh, persistent sin after profession reveals the lack of a genuine conversion. The presence of sin in the believer's life is a sensitive problem and needs explanation. John gave this exposition:

> Whosoever abideth in him sinneth not: whosoever sinneth hath not seen him, neither known him. Little children, let no man deceive you: he that doeth righteousness is righteous, even as he is righteous. He that *committeth* sin is of the devil; for the devil *sinneth* from the beginning. For this purpose the Son of God was manifested, that he might destroy the works of the devil. Who-

5 1 8 7 8

soever is born of God *doth not commit sin;* for his seed
remaineth in him: and he *cannot sin,* because he is born
of God. In this the children of God are manifest, and the
children of the devil: whosoever doeth not righteousness
is not of God, neither he that loveth not his brother (1
Jn 3:6-10).

The italicized verbs in the above passage are all in the
present tense (Greek). The present tense does not refer to
a single act of sin or to sins committed occasionally but
rather to continuous sinning. A person, really born of God
and abiding in Christ, will not sin persistently. The indwelling nature of God ("his seed") will not permit him
to do so. He will continue to sin after his conversion, but
he will sin consciously less than he did in his unsaved days.
Committing one act of adultery or murder or stealing does
not place the Christian under the scope of these verses.
How often we have heard people say, "If John Doe really
were a Christian, how could he commit adultery?" But
Christians are capable of committing adultery or any other
sin. However, if a professing Christian commits the same
sin over and over again, there is good reason to question
his salvation experience.

Eighth, perfection is never achieved in this life. After
three successful missionary journeys, Paul expressed this
ambition during his first Roman imprisonment: "That I
may know him, and the power of his resurrection, and the
fellowship of his sufferings, being made conformable unto
his death" (Phil 3:10). Here was a person who could say
that to live was Christ (Phil 1:21); Christ was Paul's life-
style, and yet, Paul knew that pure Christianity was a
growing relationship. Jesus had said, "I am come that they
might have life, and that they might have it more abund-
antly" (Jn 10:10). Paul had spiritual life; he knew that,
but he desired with all of his heart and will the abundant

life. He wanted to know the Lord Jesus in a more intimate relationship; he wanted to lean on Jesus' breast even as the beloved John did. He wanted to have an even greater victory over the temptations of the world and the sin nature through the resurrection power that lived within his life (cf. Eph 1:19–2:1). He wanted to experience that total obedience to the will of God that led Christ to the cross. He desired total self-denial. He wanted to lose his life completely in the will of God in order to find the real meaning, value, and purpose of life (Mk 8:34-35).

To this great goal, Paul added these words:

> Not as though I had already attained, either were already perfect: but I follow after, if that I may apprehend that for which also I am apprehended of Christ Jesus. Brethren, I count not myself to have apprehended: but this one thing I do, forgetting those things which are behind, and reaching forth unto those things which are before, I press toward the mark for the prize of the high calling of God in Christ Jesus (Phil 3:12-14).

Paul had not yet arrived! He wanted to know and to experience all that God had provided for him in salvation. How different this attitude is from some modern opinions. Some give the impression that they have done God a favor by accepting Christ. Some are complacent in their Christian experience, while others even feel that they have achieved sinless perfection.

Paul was still pressing on or pursuing. Christ had apprehended or arrested him on the road to Damascus (Ac 9). Christ had saved him for a purpose, and Paul wanted to apprehend that purpose. In order to do that, Paul had to do two things. He had to forget the past, because past victories do not guarantee future victories; nor do past failures guarantee future failures. Too many Christians glory in the past or worry about what could have been.

Preoccupation with the past causes a defeated, anxious life. Second, Paul wanted to reach out into the future, because to him the best was yet to be. Paul practiced the motto, "Today is the first day of the rest of your life." Paul did not expect to retire from the Christian ministry or life. God had called him to salvation and to service, and Paul was ambitious to press toward the prize of that calling.

In this life, no matter how holy you are, you will never reach ultimate perfection. Some Christians expect perfection of themselves or of others, and if they do not see it, question the respective salvation experiences. However, this is wrong. Christians should have goals, but failure to reach a certain goal should not bring the fear of loss of salvation, but rather a determination to do better the next time. John said, "My little children, these things write I unto you, that ye sin not" (1 Jn 2:1a). To sin not should be the goal of every Christian, but it is a fact that we sin daily. John knew that would be the case, so he added, "And if any man sin, we have an advocate with the Father, Jesus Christ the righteous" (1 Jn 2:1b). The great hitters of baseball bat between .300 and .350. That means that a Willie Mays or a Hank Aaron gets approximately one safe hit for every three times at bat. When the hitter goes into the batters' box, he goes there to hit. He does not try to make an out, even though he knows that he could not get a hit every time. (No one carries a 1,000 lifetime batting average!) So it is with the Christian life. We go into the batters' box to sin not, even though we know it is impossible to go throughout our life without sin. If we do sin (strike out) on one occasion, we have not lost our position within the Christian "team" or family. Confess your sin, and go out and do better the next time. Our Manager (Advocate) will give you another opportunity.

Late in his life, Paul wrote to Timothy, "This is a faithful saying, and worthy of all acceptation, that Christ Jesus came into the world to save sinners; of whom I am chief" (1 Ti 1:15). I *am* chief! He did not say, "I *was* chief." Paul never got over the fact that he was a sinner saved by God's grace and longsuffering. Even as a spiritual apostle, he still sensed that he was the chief of sinners before a holy God. The deportment of man, both before and after conversion, is not sufficient to merit eternal heaven. No man could ever keep his salvation by well doing, because he could never do enough. He could never reach that total perfection every moment of every day.

There is an obvious principle in Scripture. The closer one draws to God the more sensitive to his own sinfulness he becomes. Job said, "I have heard of thee by the hearing of the ear: but now mine eye seeth thee. Wherefore I abhor myself, and repent in dust and ashes" (Job 42:5-6). After Isaiah saw the holiness of God, he confessed, "Woe is me! for I am undone; because I am a man of unclean lips, and I dwell in the midst of a people of unclean lips: for mine eyes have seen the King, the LORD of hosts" (Is 6:5). When we compare ourselves with other preselected men, we come off pretty well; but when we compare ourselves with God, we should fall as dead men before His feet (Rev 1:17).

The point is this: desire to be holy as God is holy. But if you sin or fail one particular day, do not fear the loss of your salvation or do not become frustrated. Confess your sin, forget your sin, and reach out for the new moment to live for God. Perfection will be achieved one day, but only at the coming of Christ.

The ninth principle is that there is a difference between the spiritual position of the believer and his daily practice. Men criticize the Christian's practice, but God accepts his position in Christ. The position never changes; the practice changes daily. Men are saved or condemned because of their position. (See chaps. 1-2). Practice does not determine position; it reflects the latter. The believer's position is secure: "Because as [Christ] is, so are we in this world" (1 Jn 4:17). In practice, we are not as holy as Christ is; but in position, we are just as acceptable to God as He is. Paul called the Corinthians "saints" (1 Co 1:2); but they were not saintly but carnal. The former was their position, the latter their practice.

The finest illustration to show the difference between position and practice comes from the wilderness wanderings of the Israelites. After God had delivered the nation from Egyptian bondage, the people began their march to the promised land. When they arrived at the barrier of the Red Sea, they saw and heard the Egyptian chariots coming after them. They immediately complained to God and to Moses (Ex 14:10-12). God parted the waters, delivering the Israelites and destroying the Egyptians. The people later came to Marah and murmured against Moses because the water there was bitter (Ex 15:23-26); God made the water sweet. In the wilderness of Sin, they murmured again against Moses and Aaron because of the shortage of food (Ex 16:1-13); so God gave them manna. They came to Rephidim and chided with Moses and tempted God because they had no water to drink (Ex 17:1-7); so God miraculously produced water out of the rock. At Sinai, while Moses was on the mountain receiving the word of the Lord, the people were in the valley breaking the law (Ex 32). They made an idol, a golden calf, and worshiped it. The nation was spared judgment through the advocacy of Moses. When the people marched toward Kadesh-barnea they complained about the steady diet of manna (Num 11:1-32), so God sent quails to satisfy their appetites. Their overindulgence brought a plague from God.

At Kadesh-barnea, the people refused to trust God and voted not to enter the land (Num 13-14). Because of their unbelief, God chastised them with forty years of wandering in the wilderness, during which all of the rebellious adult Israelites perished. There was later a rebellion led by Korah (Num 16) and further complaint over the shortage of water and food (Num 20-21). Finally, the nation arrived on the plains of Moab, on the east bank of the Jordan River.

At this time, Balak the king of Moab, hired Balaam, a prophet, to curse the people of Israel. However, God said to Balaam, "Thou shalt not curse the people: for they are blessed" (Num 22:12). Later, Balaam said to Balak, "How shall I curse, whom God hath not cursed? or how shall I defy, whom the LORD hath not defied?" (Num 23:8). Balak was infuriated and cried out to Balaam, "What hast thou done unto me? I took thee to curse mine enemies, and, behold thou hast blessed them altogether" (Num 23:11). To this, Balaam responded with these paradoxical words:

> God is not a man, that he should lie; neither the son of man, that he should repent: hath he said, and shall he not do it? or hath he spoken, and shall he not make it good? Behold, I have received commandment to bless: and he hath blessed; and I cannot reverse it. He hath not beheld iniquity in Jacob, neither hath he seen perverseness in Israel: the LORD his God is with him, and the shout of a king is among them (Num 23:19-21).

"He hath not beheld iniquity in Jacob, neither hath he seen perverseness in Israel." How could Balaam say that? From Egypt to Moab, the history of Israel was that of complaining, murmuring, rebellion, and unbelief. They had even committed spiritual adultery in their idolatrous actions at Sinai. Balaam was describing the *position* of Israel, not its practice. God saw His people in its covenant relationship, the covenant that He had unconditionally promised to Abraham, Isaac, and Jacob. Their position was perfect, free from condemnation, criticism, and cursing. Their practice was terrible, and God chastised them for their sins. But, the sinful practice could never remove the secure position. As it was with Israel, so it is with Christians today; we often practice sin, but God sees no sin in us positionally. As Christ is, so are we!

The tenth principle is rather complex. If works are needed to keep salvation, then this concept is the same as becoming saved in the first place by faith and works. The Bible teaches that a man is not saved by faith *and* works. You cannot become a Christian by dual trust—trust in what Christ has done and trust in what you can do. Salvation is a gift of God based upon Christ's satisfactory sacrifice. Salvation cannot be divided into parts. When a person believes on Christ, he is not given one-third or one-half of salvation; he is given *total* salvation. To say that a man is initially saved by faith but kept saved by works is to say that salvation *does* depend upon man's effort. This position teaches that faith gives you a membership in the salvation club, but works are the necessary dues to keep up the membership. This is contrary to the following grace-faith concept of justification:

> Now to him that worketh is the reward not reckoned of grace, but of debt. But to him that worketh not, but believeth on him that justifieth the ungodly, his faith is counted for righteousness. Even as David also describeth the blessedness of the man, unto whom God imputeth righteousness without works (Ro 4:4-6).

If man must work either to obtain or to keep salvation, then God is obligated to pay salvation or at least some part of it as wages. Man then, somehow, becomes his own savior.

Paul recognized this error when he wrote, "I do not [make null and void] the grace of God: for if righteousness come by the law, then Christ is dead in vain" (Gal 2:21). If works are needed to keep salvation, then some meritorious righteousness comes by human effort. If that is so, then why did Christ die? Was He wrong when He said, "It is finished"? If works are needed to gain or to keep salvation, He should have said, "It is partially finished. Man must complete the job." Either Christ satisfied all of God's righteous demands or He satisfied none of them. Salvation, in its total sense, is either a grace gift from God secured by faith or trust alone, or it is totally secured and maintained by human effort.

Paul wrote, "Who [Christ] hath saved us, and called us with an holy calling, not according to our works, but according to his own purpose and grace, which was given us in Christ Jesus before the world began" (2 Ti 1:9). Not according to our works! These works would refer to all works, both those done before and after the salvation experience. From eternity past, God could foresee all future works done by man, but He did not save man on that basis.

This is why Paul wanted to "win Christ, And be found in him, not having mine own righteousness, which is of the law, but that which is through the faith of Christ, the righteousness which is of God by faith" (Phil 3:8-9). A person cannot be found both in Christ and in himself.

The entire book of Galatians was written to combat the Judaizing error of mixing law with grace or works with faith. Wherever Paul evangelized the Gentiles, these false teachers would come in after his departure. They would tell the new converts that faith was only the starting point and that law-keeping, including circumcision, was necessary to complete the salvation process. In essence, they were teaching that faith *and* works were necessary to secure and to maintain salvation. Paul called this a perversion of the gospel and pronounced a curse upon those who preached the error (Gal 1:7-9). He reasoned with the Galatian converts, "Are ye so foolish? having begun in the Spirit, are ye now made perfect by the flesh" (Gal 3:3)? Can the flesh (human effort) make anything perfect? Certainly not. Works cannot complete what faith has started. The faith that saved continues to trust. That is the essence of saving faith. It cannot be turned off or on at will.

Paul warned the Galatians, "Behold, I Paul say unto you, that if ye be circumcised, Christ shall profit you nothing" (Gal 5:2). If a person believes that he must add works (circumcision, baptism, daily obedience, etc.) to faith in Christ in order to have total salvation, he has actually negated for himself the value of Christ's death and resurrection. Either a person completely trusts Christ for all of salvation, or he is not trusting at all. It is not a joint proposition. You do not trust Christ for 99 percent of your salvation and your works for the other 1 percent.

Paul developed a clever allegory to illustrate this point (Gal 4:19-31). Abraham had two sons, Isaac and Ishmael. Isaac was a child of promise, born of the free woman, Sarah. Ishmael was the child of human effort, born to the bondwoman, Hagar. Sarah represents grace and faith; Hagar symbolizes law and works. Christians are like Isaac, the children of promise. What is Paul trying to say here? A person cannot be born of two mothers. As a person could not be born of Sarah and Hagar at the same time, so a sinner cannot be born again both of faith and of works. Truly saved people are born out of simple trust in what God has promised and provided through Christ. If a person believes that works are necessary to keep salvation, in essence, he may be trusting self for his salvation. If he is, then he is like Ishmael and will not receive the promise.

Actually, he is not saved, but is still under bondage to sin.

The future fulfillment of God's promises to Israel guarantees the completion of God's purpose for each Christian. (This is the eleventh and final principle.) Some have regarded Paul's discourse on Israel (Ro 9-11) as parenthetical material, inserted between God's program for the Christian (chaps. 1-8) and the believer's daily responsibilities (chaps. 12-16). However, this is not the case. Paul was anticipating a question that the Roman Gentile Christians could possibly raise: "How can we Gentile believers trust God to complete His announced purpose for us (predestination, calling, justification, and glorification) when He has not yet fulfilled His program for Israel?" Perhaps God would set them aside just as He had set Israel aside, they reasoned. Can we be sure that God is working out all things for our good? These were fair questions and needed to be answered.

The nation of Israel was indeed a special, privileged nation.

> Who are Israelites; to whom pertaineth the adoption, and the glory, and the covenants, and the giving of the law, and the service of God, and the promises; Whose are the fathers, and of whom as concerning the flesh Christ came, who is over all, God blessed for ever. Amen (Ro 9:4-5).

God had made four unconditional covenants with them: Abrahamic (Gen 12:1-3), Palestinian (Deu 30:1-10), Davidic (2 Sa 7:11-17), and the New (Jer 31:31-37). These covenants outlined God's purposes for the nation and guaranteed their future. They were to be the greatest nation on the earth and were to possess all of Palestine. Their kingdom would last forever. They would be both spiritually redeemed from sin and physically redeemed from their enemies. *But*, at the writing of Romans, they were not enjoying the fulfillment of these promises.

The nation, for the most part, was not saved at this time (Ro 10:1). Paul desired and prayed for their salvation, and there were a few who received the gospel, "a remnant according to the election of grace" (11:5). But, to the natural observer, Israel had been rejected by God. Her glory was in the past but not in the future. To this inference, Paul replied,

> I say then, Have they stumbled that they should fall? God forbid: but rather through their fall salvation is come unto the Gentiles, for to provoke them to jealousy. Now if the fall of them be the riches of the world, and the diminishing of them the riches of the Gentiles; how much more their fulness (11:11-12)?

There was a divine purpose behind Israel's unbelief; the new age of Gentile blessing, the church age, was made possible. The nation had fallen or stumbled, but it was not a permanent fall or rejection. Israel would yet experience the "fulness" of God's program for her.

When the fullness of the Gentiles (the church age) is over, then the partial, temporary spiritual blindness of Israel will be lifted (11:25). Israel will then be saved and will experience the complete fulfillment of God's covenant purposes (11:26-27).

Paul then came to this marvelous conclusion: "As concerning the gospel, they are enemies for your sakes: but as touching the election, they are beloved for the fathers' sakes. For the gifts and calling of God are without repentance" (11:28-29). They were *enemies* yet *beloved!* How strange! Paul said that the Jews "killed the Lord Jesus, and their own prophets, and have persecuted us; and they please not God, and are contrary to all men: Forbidding us to speak to the Gentiles that they might be saved, to fill up their sins alway" (1 Th 2:15-16). If any people deserved to lose their privileged position, it was and is the Jews. They committed every sin and broke every law in the book. *But*, they have not lost their covenant position! Why? They were loved and elected in the fathers. The fulfillment of God's promises to Abraham was not based upon his future faithfulness or that of his descendants, but upon the integrity of God's Word. That is why Paul concluded, "For the gifts and calling of God are without repentance" (Ro 11:29). God is not an Indian giver; He does not take back what He gives. He will complete the purpose of His calling.

Paul wrote, "God hath not cast away his people which he foreknew" (Ro 11:2). In spite of Israel's sin, God will give her all that He has promised. In spite of your sin, God will conform you to the image of His dear Son (Ro 8:29). In practice, you may be an "enemy" of God in your worldliness (Ja 4:4), but since you are chosen in him before the foundation of the world (Eph 1:4), you are beloved for Christ's sake. The fulfillment of God's purpose for Israel should be an encouragement to you that He will do all that He has promised to do for you.

There is no better way to end this chapter than with Paul's benediction:

O the depth of the riches both of the wisdom and knowledge of God! how unsearchable are his judgments, and his ways past finding out! For who hath known the mind of the Lord? or who hath been his counsellor? Or who hath first given to him, and it shall be recompensed unto him again? For of him, and through him, and to him, are all things: to whom be glory forever. Amen (Ro 11:33-36).

5

What About Those Problem Passages?

NO DOCTRINE OF SCRIPTURE is immune from questions or problems. When finite men try to understand the ways of an infinite God, it should be expected that some difficulties would arise. There are some divine mysteries that will always be hidden to man. Moses wrote, "The secret things belong unto the LORD our God: but those things which are revealed belong unto us and to our children for ever, that we may do all the words of this law" (Deu 29:29).

Doctrinal problems within revealed truth many times arise because of poor translation or faulty interpretation. In some cases, the English text may be ambiguous, but a knowledge of the Greek supporting text may clearly solve the problem. Men are forever taking texts out of their contexts, failing to see the meaning of a verse in the midst of its surrounding passage. Men form doctrines on isolated texts without any regard for the teaching of Scripture elsewhere. In some passages, there can be honest disagreement because of the lack of sufficient information to make a firm judgment.

What are some typical scriptural problems? Evangelicals will agree that God created the world and that organic evolution is erroneous, but when did He create? Was the original creation judged because of satanic, angelic sin and later reconditioned for man's habitation? How could the

omniscient Son of God become man and learn (Lk 2:52)?
Did Christ die for the sin of the entire world or just for
that of the elect? Will Jesus Christ come for the church
before or after the tribulation? And, of course, can Christians lose their salvation?

It must be remembered that there is unity and harmony
within the Scriptures. The New Testament does not contradict the Old Testament, nor do the New Testament
writers contradict each other. The Bible does not teach
two opposing viewpoints. Both could possibly be wrong,
but certainly, both cannot be right at the same time.
Problem passages must be interpreted in the light of clear
passages, never vice versa.

When it comes to the doctrine of eternal security, there
are several problem passages. These can be classified into
different categories.

First, some passages refer to unsaved professors of salvation, rather than to genuine possessors. Dr. Arthur Wil-
liams, an excellent Bible teacher, used to tell his students,
"Don't call me a professor; call me a possessor!" People
can say that they are saved when they are not (cf. Ja
2:14-26). Jesus ended the Sermon on the Mount with this
warning:

> Not every one that saith unto me, Lord, Lord, shall
> enter into the kingdom of heaven; but he that doeth the
> will of my Father which is in heaven. Many will say to
> me in that day, Lord, Lord, have we not prophesied in
> thy name? and in thy name have cast out devils? and in
> thy name done many wonderful works? And then will I
> profess unto them, I never knew you: depart from me, ye
> that work iniquity (Mt 7:21-23).

These people had done "Christian" service but were not
even saved. In fact, their good works were really works of
iniquity. Jesus said that He *never* knew them. Now, if

these people had been genuine Christians at one time and had subsequently lost their salvation, Jesus could not have used the word *never*. He would have had to say, "I once knew you, but now I don't." But, He did not say that. This means that there never was a time when this crowd entered into a living, personal relationship with Jesus Christ. He did not deny that they had done these works of service in His name; He denied that He knew them personally. The Lord knows His sheep, them that are His, and these did not belong to Him (Jn 10:27; 2 Ti 2:19). They were false sheep. There are many people today, active in Christian church circles, who have substituted activity for regenerated living. They are not saved, although they think so.

In His sermon on the bread of life, Jesus challenged the people to desire spiritual bread (life) rather than physical bread. He wanted the multitude to receive Him by faith. What was their response? John wrote, "Many therefore of his disciples, when they had heard this, said, This is an hard saying; who can hear it?" (John 6:60).

To their doubt and perplexity, Jesus replied,

> It is the spirit that quickeneth; the flesh profiteth nothing: the words that I speak unto you, they are spirit, and they are life. But there are some of you that believe not. For Jesus knew from the beginning who they were that believed not, and who should betray him. And he said, Therefore said I unto you, that no man can come unto me, except it were given unto him of my Father. From that time many of his disciples went back, and walked no more with him (Jn 6:63-66).

It was possible to be a disciple and yet not be a believer. In its basic meaning, a disciple is simply a learner. These people followed the Lord out of academic curiosity. They liked to hear Him speak, especially when He spoke out against the religious establishment of the Pharisees and Sadducees. They knew that He was a miracle worker because they had eaten of the multiplied fish and bread, but they had never believed on Him. Jesus knew that and told them so. They had not been drawn to Christ by the Father. They had come to Christ out of self-interest, rather than by Spirit conviction. These disciples did not lose their salvation; they never actually had it. They professed, but they did not possess.

This was the same problem within Israel. Paul wrote, "For they are not all Israel, which are of Israel: Neither, because they are the seed of Abraham, are they all children" (Ro 9:6b-7). A true Israelite is one who is both a physical and a spiritual child of Abraham. Many Israelites professed to be free children of God (Jn 8:33-45), but they were still under the bondage of sin. So it is with Christian homes and churches today. Children born into Christian homes could manifest for years the outward signs or characteristics of Christian living (reading the Bible, praying, going to church), and yet not have the life of Christ within. Many Jewish people prayed, read the Old Testament, and sacrificed in the temple, and yet Paul called them unsaved. Profession is not a substitute for possession, nor the outward for the internal.

A second group of difficult passages deals with false, unsaved, religious teachers within Christendom. Jesus said, "Beware of false prophets, which come to you in sheep's clothing, but inwardly they are ravening wolves" (Mt 7:15). Wolves that look like sheep! There *are* men who deliberately deceive for personal gain. Paul gave this description:

> For such are false apostles, deceitful workers, transforming themselves into the apostles of Christ. And no marvel; for Satan himself is transformed into an angel of

light. Therefore it is no great thing if his ministers also be transformed as the ministers of righteousness; whose end shall be according to their works (2 Co 11:13-15).

They are ministers of righteousness, but they are spiritually unrighteous. Satan may appear as an angel of light, but he is full of darkness. In Paul's day, these false teachers were accepted by some churches as genuine apostles, but Paul identified them as unsaved deceivers.

Paul warned the Ephesian elders, "For I know this, that after my departing shall grievous wolves enter in among you, not sparing the flock. Also of your own selves shall men arise, speaking perverse things, to draw away disciples after them" (Ac 20:29-30). Unsaved church members ("of your own selves") can rise to prominence and power. Their words and actions testify to the fact that they have the same character as the infiltrating false teachers. John described these antichristian preachers thus: "They went out from us, but they were not of us; for if they had been of us, they would no doubt have continued with us: but they went out, that they might be made manifest that they were not all of us" (1 Jn 2:19). These false teachers were once identified with the Christian group ("they went out *from* us"), but they were not really saved ("they were not *of* us"). The fact that they no longer continued with the Christian family demonstrated their unregenerate condition. Once these false teachers are uncovered, there should be no church or personal fellowship with them. Paul wrote,

> Now I beseech you, brethren, mark them which cause divisions and offences contrary to the doctrine which ye have learned; and avoid them. For they that are such serve not our Lord Jesus Christ, but their own belly; and by good words and fair speeches deceive the hearts of the simple (Ro 16:17-18).

John cautioned the elect lady not to give them any opportunity to spread their false doctrine (2 Jn 7-11).

Peter predicted, "But there were false prophets also among the people, even as there shall be false teachers among you, who privily shall bring in damnable heresies, even denying the Lord that bought them and bring upon themselves swift destruction" (2 Pe 2:1). Were these teachers saved or unsaved? They are called *false* teachers, but some still regard them as Christians who lost their salvation through moral and doctrinal heresy. The following passage is cited as their proof:

> While they promise them liberty, they themselves are the servants of corruption: for of whom a man is overcome, of the same is he brought in bondage. For if after they have escaped the pollutions of the world through the knowledge of the Lord and Saviour Jesus Christ, they are again entangled therein, and overcome, the latter end is worse with them than the beginning. For it had been better for them not to have known the way of righteousness, than, after they have known it, to turn from the holy commandment delivered unto them. But it is happened unto them according to the true proverb, the dog is turned to his own vomit again; and the sow that was washed to her wallowing in the mire (2 Pe 2:19-22).

At first glance, this passage seems to hold difficulties for the adherents of eternal security. They escaped the pollutions of the *world*, but did they escape the divine wrath of the lake of fire? They knew the *way* of righteousness, but did they receive the *gift* of divine righteousness? They turned from the *commandment*, but did they turn from a position in Christ? The proverb helps to solve the problem. The dog returned to that which defiled its stomach. The hog returned to the mudhole after its bath. You can take a pig out of the mud, give it a bath, put a ribbon on its tail, take it to the county fair, and win a blue ribbon; but when that pig is given the opportunity, it will return to slopping in the mud. Why? Because its nature has not changed. A hog is a hog whether it is clean or dirty. These false teachers, like many professing Christians, had enjoyed the fringe benefits of Christianity apart from the real life of Christ.

In this world, the best life (physical, mental, and emotional) is that practiced by the Christian. Those who practice such great sins as sexual lust, drinking, smoking, and drugs age fast and become dissipated. These false teachers practiced the Christian life for a while, but they did not possess the spiritual position of the regenerated person. Their judgment in the lake of fire will be more severe because their responsibility for rejecting more truth was greater. Note these descriptive phrases: "unjust . . . walk after the flesh in the lust of uncleanness . . . Presumptuous . . . selfwilled . . . natural brute beasts . . . shall receive the reward of unrighteousness . . . Spots, blemishes . . . Having eyes full of adultery . . . cannot cease from sin . . . cursed children . . . wells without water . . . to whom the mist of darkness is reserved forever" (2 Pe 2:9-17). In fact, these teachers even denied the reality of the second coming of Jesus Christ and the subsequent judgment of the world by fire (2 Pe 3:3-4). This catalog befits a person who has always been unsaved, not one who experienced genuine salvation in Christ and then lost it.

A third group of problem passages involves doctrinal error or defection. As mentioned before, orthodox doctrine is the basis of genuine faith. Sincere belief based upon error cannot save anyone. Many so-called losers of salvation never really had a correct doctrinal foundation. Their faith was based upon their own concept of what should be believed rather than upon the correct scriptural position.

Paul predicted,

> Now the Spirit speaketh expressly, that in the latter times some shall depart from the faith, giving heed to seducing spirits, and doctrines of devils; Speaking lies in hypocrisy; having their conscience seared with a hot iron, Forbidding to marry, and commanding to abstain from meats (1 Ti 4:1-3).

This was not departure from personal faith, but from *the* faith. This refers to the body of doctrinal truth embraced by Christians as the necessary foundation for genuine conversion and spiritual fellowship. Jude told his readers to "contend for the faith which was once delivered unto the saints" (Jude 3). The orthodox doctrinal position of the apostolic church had already been defined before the writing of Jude's epistle. Only the writings of John the apostle remained to be penned after this time. Nothing could be added to or subtracted from *the* faith which was *once* delivered. The need was to defend what had already been revealed and to judge new teachers in the light of this revealed truth. Jude's opponents distorted the grace of God and denied the deity of Jesus Christ (v. 4). Timothy's adversaries were satanically controlled hypocrites and doctrinal apostates. No genuine Christian ever defects from the doctrinal fundamentals of the faith.

There was some fuzzy doctrinal thinking in Corinth. Paul was concerned about the faith of those Greek converts from pagan idolatry and philosophy. Did their faith rest upon a true or a faulty doctrinal concept? He wrote,

> Moreover, brethren, I declare unto you the gospel which I preached unto you, which also ye have received, and wherein ye stand;
>
> By which also ye are saved, if ye keep in memory what I preached unto you, unless ye have believed in vain (1 Co 15:1-2).

The problem rests upon the conditional clause (introduced by *if*). Did Paul mean that they would keep their salvation as long as they maintained their faith ("if ye keep in memory")? Or, is something else meant here? What does it mean to believe "in vain"? The gospel message includes both the crucifixion and resurrection of Christ. It is impossible to become a Christian without believing that Jesus rose from the grave in a real body that was seen and touched by many (1 Co 15:3-11). Apparently the Corinthians believed this doctrine, and yet some of them were denying the reality of their own future bodily resurrection. Paul questioned them, "Now if Christ be preached that he rose from the dead, how say some among you that there is no resurrection of the dead" (1 Co 15:12)? To deny the future resurrection of human beings must include the denial of past resurrections, including that of Jesus Christ (1 Co 15:13). You cannot have one without the other. Paul then argued, "And if Christ be not risen, then is our preaching vain, and your faith is also vain" (1 Co 15:14). A crucified, nonresurrected Christ cannot save anyone. What was the purpose of Christ's resurrection? Was it not to guarantee everlasting life? You cannot have eternal life without resurrection life. Notice how Jesus combined them. "And this is the will of him that sent me, that everyone which seeth the Son, and believeth on him, may have everlasting life: and I will raise him up at the last day" (Jn 6:42). Denial of the resurrection strips the gospel message of its necessary content. It is empty, like a nut having a shell but no kernel. Paul also argued: "And if Christ be not raised, your faith is vain; ye are yet in your sins. Then they also which are fallen asleep in Christ are perished" (1 Co 15:17-18). If there is no resurrection of the dead, then their faith had no purpose or meaning; it was useless. Paul then sounded the triumphant note: "But now is Christ risen from the

dead, and become the firstfruits of them that slept" (1 Co
15:20). Jesus *did* rise from the dead; therefore, we too will
rise from the dead. Thus, to believe "in vain" is not only
to deny the future resurrection of believers but also to
deny the bodily resurrection of Jesus Christ. This kind of
faith cannot save anyone. Paul was simply giving the Corinthians a doctrinal examination. What was the exact
content of their faith? If it included both the resurrection
of Christ and that of themselves, they were genuinely
saved. They could not admit one and deny the other; thus
if their faith included the denial of the resurrection concept, they were not really saved.

Paul warned against a "salvation" that was dependent
upon both faith and human effort:

> Stand fast therefore in the liberty wherewith Christ
> hath made us free, and be not entangled again with the
> yoke of bondage. Behold, I Paul say unto you, that if ye
> be circumcised, Christ shall profit you nothing. For I
> testify again to every man that is circumcised, that he is a
> debtor to do the whole law. Christ is become of no
> effect unto you, whosoever of you are justified by the law;
> ye are fallen from grace (Gal 5:1-4).

The problem phrase is, "Ye are fallen from grace." To
many, to fall from grace means to lose one's salvation. But,
is this passage teaching about the keeping or the losing of
salvation? No! Paul is answering the question, How does
a person gain salvation? Does he only trust Christ, or must
he add some human effort? Paul cautioned against adding
anything. In that day, the Judaizers attempted to add circumcision and law-keeping as necessary concomitants. To
do so would only negate the value of Christ's death and
resurrection to them. There are only two approaches to
God. A man can either try to be justified by the law (doing something) or he can be justified by grace (trusting

Christ). A man must choose between the human standard and the divine principle. There is no third approach where man can merge trust with effort. To fall from grace means to forsake God's approach for man's approach. No one can be justified by human effort. "There is a way which seemeth right unto a man, but the end thereof are the ways of death" (Pr 14:12). Actually, the person who insists upon works as necessary to gain initial salvation or to gain final salvation is the one who has "fallen" from grace. He has not really trusted Christ in the fullest sense of the word.

Some people confuse loss of reward with loss of salvation. The judgment seat of Christ is not an event where Christians could possibly lose their salvation. It is a time when rewards are either given or withheld. Paul wrote,

> Every man's work shall be made manifest: for the day shall declare it, because it shall be revealed by fire; and the fire shall try every man's work of what sort it is. If any man's work abide which he hath built thereupon, he shall receive a reward. If any man's work shall be burned, he shall suffer loss: but he himself shall be saved; yet so as by fire (1 Co 3:13-15).

At this event, which takes place in heaven after Christ's coming, He will examine the *works* of the believer, not his position. The position is secure because it rests upon the foundation of Christ. The fire does not try the person, only his works. This is not a Protestant purgatory. Quality work will be rewarded; inferior work will be burned. The believer will indeed suffer loss, but loss of what? Of salvation? No. Paul quickly added, "But he himself shall be saved; yet so as by fire." The believer will have lost what could have been. His was a saved life, but it was also wasted. Saved, yet so as by fire, but *still* saved.

Some passages describe a weakened spiritual condition. The concept of Christian liberty in nonmoral issues has been greatly misunderstood and exercised improperly. It has always been a moot, sensitive area. Too often the sins of suspicion and false accusation have accompanied it. Christians, churches and evangelical colleges have debated what the standards of Christian conduct should be. Is it right or wrong to attend movies? To watch movies on television? To dance? To read contemporary novels? To wear cosmetics? To wear short skirts or long hair? To engage in mixed bathing? Hard feelings have developed over the answers given to these questions. Since there are no direct biblical passages dealing with these exact contemporary situations, the problem is even more compounded. It can only be solved by a yielded Christian, sensitive to the direction of the Holy Spirit and to the needs of his fellow believers, and willing to apply the principles of God's Word to twentieth-century living. This is why Paul gave so much attention to the problem (Ro 14-15; 1 Co 8-10). He wanted Christians to edify, not to destroy, one another. He wanted them to build each other up, not tear each one down. Read his analysis of the problem:

> But meat commendeth us not to God: for neither, if we eat, are we the better; neither, if we eat not, are we the worse. But take heed lest by any means this liberty of your's become a stumblingblock to them that are weak. For if any man see thee which hast knowledge sit at meat in the idol's temple, shall not the conscience of him which is weak be emboldened to eat those things which are offered to idols; And through thy knowledge shall the weak brother perish, for whom Christ died? But when ye sin so against the brethren, and wound their weak conscience, ye sin against Christ (1 Co 8:8-12).

How does the weak brother *perish?* If a person abuses the privileges of Christian liberty given to him by the Saviour, he puts a stumbling block before his fellow Christian. He wounds his brother's conscience. He causes his brother to do something which the latter has no right to do in the area of Christian liberty. Such an action will cause the weak brother to have a guilty conscience. He will feel defeated and discouraged. His Christian growth will suffer a set-back, not because of the temptations of the world or of the devil, but because of the deeds of an indifferent brother in Christ. Paul warned, "But if thy brother be grieved with thy meat, now walkest thou not charitably. Destroy not him with thy meat, for whom Christ died" (Ro 14:15). The brother perishes or is destroyed when he observes a fellow Christian doing that which he feels is wrong and becomes depressed over it or when he participates in an activity which God has not approved for his life. God does not destroy him; another believer does. These passages do not teach the loss of salvation; they point out the loss of spiritual growth and the loss of spiritual confidence in other Christians. In that sense, his life is destroyed.

Some passages teach loss of privilege or Christian service opportunities, not loss of salvation. God not only calls men to salvation but also to service for Him. Through sin and carnality, a Christian can forfeit his area of spiritual influence. Paul even expressed this concern:

> I therefore so run, not as uncertainly, so fight I, not as one that beateth the air: But I keep under my body, and bring it into subjection: lest that by any means, when I have preached to others, I myself should be a castaway (1 Co 9:26-27).

Paul looked upon Christian service as a race. In order to complete and to win the race, one must be in good spiritual shape, and he must run according to the divine rules. Paul did not desire mediocrity, but mastery. In the great Olympic games, men strive for the gold, silver, and bronze medals, but Paul wanted to win an incorruptible crown. This crown is not eternal life, because men do not gain eternal life through effort or service. This crown is given to the Christian who practices the disciplined, spiritual life in order to win others to Christ.

Paul's desire was to be made all things to all men that he might by all means save some (1 Co 9:22). Paul did not want to minister to others apart from ministering to himself. How tragic it would be for a servant of God to teach others how to live and yet not practice the truth himself. It is one thing to run the race; it is another to do it according to the rules. Paul did not want to finish his ministry and then be disqualified at the judgment seat of Christ. He did not want to be a castaway, that is, disapproved of God but rather approved. In some cases, the public manifestation of divine disapproval can come in this life. Because of sin, a pastor could lose forever his opportunity to shepherd a flock. Deacons are not voted back into office because the people lack confidence in them. Loss of service privilege should not be mistaken for loss of salvation.

On the night before His crucifixion, Jesus said to His disciples, "I am the vine, ye are the branches: He that abideth in me, and I in him, the same bringeth forth much fruit: for without me ye can do nothing" (Jn 15:5). Christ was speaking about fruit-bearing, not about the retention of salvation. This entire metaphor must be seen against the background of that purpose. The fact that they were branches establishes that they were genuine believers because they were formed out of the life of the vine. Now, as branches, it was their responsibility to permit the life of the vine to flow through them for the production of fruit. No branch can produce fruit apart from its living, organic connection to the vine. Jesus wanted to impress this truth upon the disciples. Apart from Him, they were incapable of doing anything for God. They were to abide in Him, in His Word, and in His love. Their responsibility was to be completely yielded to Him.

When a believer is full of self and rebellion, he restricts the flow of the vine—or Christ—through him. People are unable to see the manifestation of Christ in and through his life. What happens to this type of person? Jesus said, "If a man abide not in me, he is cast forth as a branch, and is withered; and men gather them, and cast them into the fire, and they are burned" (Jn 15:6). A branch that no longer lets the life of the vine flow through it turns from green to brown. When the vine-dresser sees that the branch will no longer bear fruit, he prunes it and throws it on a pile where it will dry and later be used as kindling for a fire. The branch has been removed from its fruit-bearing position. So it is with the unyielded Christian. God will remove him from his privileged place of fruit-bearing. The only purpose that a Christian has in this life is to manifest Christ. If he no longer wills to do that, then God has a perfect right to prune him. The person could be publicly discredited and lose any area of spiritual influence that he might have had, or, God may choose to take him home in premature physical death. There is no indication here of hellfire. Men can gather dried branches for a fire, but men have no part in casting other men into the lake of fire.

Jesus warned the Ephesian church, "Remember therefore from whence thou art fallen, and repent, and do the first works; or else I will come unto thee quickly, and will remove thy candlestick out of his place, except thou repent" (Rev 2:5). This was addressed to a church, not to an individual. The Ephesian church was orthodox but cold. Love for Christ and for Christians no longer possessed it (Rev 2:4; cf. Eph 1:15). If they would not repent of this sin, then their candlestick, their opportunity to bear light for Christ in a dark, godless world, would be removed. This is exactly what happened. In the first century, the key local church of Asia Minor was located in Ephesus. Paul labored there for three years; it was the home base for missionary expansion into that region (modern Turkey). With the break-up of the Roman empire and the advent of Islam, the Ephesian light disappeared. Today, Turkey belongs to the Muslim world and the evangelical witness in Ephesus has vanished. Its opportunity to serve as a local church was taken away.

Paul's olive tree analogy has been used by some to teach the loss of salvation:

> And if some of the branches be broken off, and thou, being a wild olive tree, wert graffed in among them, and with them partakest of the root and fatness of the olive tree; Boast not against the branches. But if thou boast, thou bearest not the root, but the root thee. Thou wilt say then, The branches were broken off, that I might be graffed in. Well; because of unbelief they were broken off, and thou standest by faith. Be not highminded, but fear: For if God spared not the natural branches, take heed lest he also spare not thee. Behold therefore the goodness and severity of God: on them which fell, severity; but toward thee, goodness, if thou continue in his goodness: otherwise thou also shalt be cut off. And they also, if they abide not still in unbelief, shall be graffed in: for God is able to graff them in again. For if thou wert cut out of the olive tree which is wild by nature, and were graffed contrary to nature into a good olive tree: how much more shall these, which be the natural branches, be graffed into their own olive tree? (Ro 11:17-24).

According to them, "to be cut off" means to lose one's salvation, but such an interpretation does an injustice to the context. Paul, here, is harmonizing the spiritual blindness of Israel with the age of the church, a special time of Gentile blessing which he calls "the fulness of the Gentiles" (Ro 11:25). From the call of Abraham to the death of Jesus Christ, Israel (the natural branches) was the vehicle through which God manifested His program and blessed the world. From the death of Christ to the present, the church, comprised of both Gentiles and Jews, occupies that position. (The wild olive branches represent the majority of Gentiles in the church.) The olive tree represents God's gracious program throughout the ages. Paul was warning the Gentiles not to be spiritually proud. The period of Gentile blessing only began after Israel rejected her Messiah and lost her position of prominence. However, Israel will again occupy the central place within God's program during the great tribulation and the millennial kingdom. The "grafting" and "cutting" of this passage do not refer to personal gaining and losing of salvation, but to the usage of Israel and the Gentile church within God's dispensational program for the ages.

Some confuse accountability with loss of salvation. God said to Ezekiel, "When I say unto the wicked, Thou shalt surely die; and thou givest him not warning, nor speakest to warn the wicked from his wicked way, to save his life; the same wicked man shall die in his iniquity; but his blood will I require at thine hand" (Eze 3:18; cf. 33:8). How could blood be required at Ezekiel's hand? Would Ezekiel also die physically or be sent to hell if he failed to warn the wicked? Certainly not the latter. If a person ends up in hell, he is there because he consciously rejected God's truth. He is not there because someone failed to witness to him; man is responsible before God for his own sins. God had made Ezekiel a spiritual watchman unto the house of Israel (Eze 3:17), especially to the Jewish captives in Babylon before the destruction of Jerusalem. The "death" in this passage may refer to imminent physical death at the hands of the Babylonians. Both Jeremiah and Ezekiel called the people to repentance and to submission to Babylon as God's will for Israel. The people would not believe that God would permit the Babylonians to destroy them, therefore they persisted in their stubborn unbelief. Those who resisted the prophetic message died in the siege of Jerusalem either from hunger or by the sword. The people could not blame Ezekiel; he had spoken the truth. If he had failed to give them the divine message, he would have been held accountable for failure to discharge his responsibility, but only that.

When Pilate washed his hands at the trial of Christ, he shouted, "I am innocent of the blood of this just person: see ye to it" (Mt 27:24). He was disclaiming any responsibility for the crucifixion. The people replied: "His blood be on us, and on our children" (Mt 27:25). The crowd freely accepted the responsibility for the death of Jesus. In fact, they even imposed it upon their descendants. And yet, many of those Jewish children have come to a saving knowledge of Christ in this age, and Israel as a nation will be saved at the second coming of Christ. The "blood" upon them did not secure eternal doom for them, but it did bring the physical judgment of God upon them both at the destruction of Jerusalem by the Romans and by anti-Semitic persecutions throughout the centuries.

Paul declared his freedom from accountability to the Ephesian elders at Miletus: "Wherefore I take you to record this day, that I am pure from the blood of all men. For I have not shunned to declare unto you all the counsel of God" (Ac 20:26-27). Paul had fulfilled his apostolic duties by not only evangelizing the city of Ephesus but by also teaching the converts *all* of the divine counsel. This involved proper teaching of doctrinal truths and practical

Christian living. He had completed his moral obligation to both sinner and saint. No one could charge him for preaching partial truth. If Paul had won people to Christ but had failed to teach them, he would have been accountable to God for failure to do all of the Great Commission. He could lose rewards for this; he could lose future service privileges over this; but he could never lose his salvation.

Are today's Christians just as accountable as an Old Testament prophet or a New Testament apostle? We do have responsibilities, but *nowhere* in Scripture does God threaten us with "blood upon us" for failure to complete our tasks. Because of their unique authoritative position, these warnings may have pertained only to Ezekiel and to Paul.

Some people confuse initial confession with daily confession. In the ordination address to His twelve disciples, Jesus spoke about two opposite responses to their preaching ministry:

> Whosoever therefore shall confess me before men, him will I confess also before my Father which is in heaven. But whosoever shall deny me before men, him will I also deny before my Father which is in heaven (Mt 10:32-33).

Christ was not talking about the future confession or denial of the twelve; He was referring to the Jewish listeners. He had already mentioned that some might not receive them into their houses (Mt 10:14). He had warned them of wolves who would persecute them (Mt 10:16-19). He had predicted that families would be divided over their message (Mt 10:21; cf. 10:34-37). Their preaching would divide men into two groups: the confessors and the deniers (the saved and the unsaved). This is initial confession unto salvation, the same type later described by Paul:

> But what saith it? The word is nigh thee, even in thy

> mouth, and in thy heart: that is, the word of faith, which
> we preach; That if thou shalt confess with thy mouth the
> Lord Jesus, and shalt believe in thine heart that God hath
> raised him from the dead, thou shalt be saved. For with
> the heart man believeth unto righteousness; and with the
> mouth confession is made unto salvation. For the scrip-
> ture saith, Whosoever believeth on him shall not be
> ashamed (Ro 10:8-11).

Genuine heart belief will express itself through the confession of the mouth. A truly saved person will be happy
to confess his confidence in Christ. The Spirit of God will
overcome the person's shyness or natural reluctance to
speak in public. Confession is not a prerequisite to salvation but the direct result of it. Just as the confession is
audible, so is the denial. Out of the abundance of the
heart the mouth speaks. If a person consciously repudiates
the truth of the gospel message, then he will be rejected
by Christ before the Father. Christ was speaking about a
crisis decision to accept or to reject, not about daily re-
affirmation of one's faith.

Some passages have been dispensationally misapplied.
Many untaught and immature Christians fear the unpardonable sin. They do not know what it is, but they are
afraid that, if they commit it, they will lose their salvation.
The only place where the unpardonable sin is mentioned
and described is in the gospels, never in the epistles or in
the Old Testament. At a pivotal point in His ministry to
Israel, Jesus said,

> Wherefore I say unto you, All manner of sin and blas-
> phemy shall be forgiven unto men: but the blasphemy
> against the Holy Ghost shall not be forgiven unto men.
> And whosoever speaketh a word against the Son of man,
> it shall be forgiven him: but whosoever speaketh against
> the Holy Ghost, it shall not be forgiven him, neither in

this world, neither in the world to come (Mt 12:31-32).
That is some warning, but to whom was it spoken? Look
at the background of this passage. Jesus had presented
Himself to Israel as her king and had offered the kingdom,
promised to David but destroyed by the Babylonians (586
B.C.). He had authenticated His claim and message by
His virgin birth; by the correct Jewish geneological background; by the way His early life was confirmed by the
Old Testament; by the pronouncements of His forerunner,
John the Baptist; by His sinless life; by His ability to legis-
late (Sermon on the Mount); and by His miracles. A few
of the people accepted Him as the Jewish Messiah; the
great majority was still undecided. The religious leaders
(Pharisees, Sadducees, and priests) greatly opposed Him
and looked for ways to justify their rejection of Him and
to belittle Christ before the people. In fact, they had already determined to destroy Him (Mt 12:14). At this
time, Jesus cast out a demon which had caused blindness
and dumbness in a person. The observing multitude immediately reacted: "Is not this the son of David?" (Mt
12:23). They were not sure, but the miracle had almost
convinced them.

It was then that the Pharisees gave their public, official
explanation of the person of Jesus and of His ministry.
They said, "This fellow doth not cast out devils, but by
Beelzebub the prince of the devils" (Mt 12:24). The
Pharisees had just called Jesus an insane demoniac. They
did not deny the miracle. They admitted that Jesus had
supernatural power, but they claimed that Jesus worked
by Satan and not by the Spirit of God. Jesus charged them
with the unpardonable sin. They were not forgiven that
sin, either during the rest of Christ's earthly ministry or
during the church age which began at Pentecost after His
death and resurrection. These leaders were the same ones

who later repudiated and persecuted the apostles in Jerusalem.

Can the unpardonable sin be committed today? The historical approach to the problem would say no, because those historical circumstances are not in existence today. However, someone could believe today that Jesus did perform miracles then but by the power of Satan; if this were the case, then that person would be guilty of that terrible sin. Today, though, most liberals simply deny the existence of demons or Satan, the personality of the Holy Spirit, and the reality of Christ's miracles. They dismiss His nature miracles as pious legend or myth and relegate His healings to psychosomatic suggestion.

Another plausible interpretation of this difficult passage states that the unpardonable sin is the continual rejection of Jesus Christ as Lord and Saviour. To reject Christ during one's lifetime and to die without faith in Him is the one sin that will condemn an unbeliever forever. Paul said that God reconciled "the world unto himself, not imputing their trespasses unto them" (2 Co 5:19). The issue between God and man today is the *Son* problem, not *sin*. Just as the Pharisees disbelieved stubbornly, so a person today can harden himself against the claims of Christ. Solomon warned, "He, that being often reproved hardeneth his neck, shall suddenly be destroyed, and that without remedy" (Pr 29:1).

In either interpretation, though, the unpardonable sin can only be committed by an unsaved person. The Pharisees certainly represented that class. There is no scriptural support that this sin could ever be done by a genuine Christian.

In the same context as the unpardonable sin is another greatly misunderstood passage. Christ told the Jews:

When the unclean spirit is gone out of a man, he

walketh through dry places, seeking rest, and findeth none. Then he saith, I will return into my house from whence I came out; and when he is come, he findeth it empty, swept, and garnished. Then goeth he, and taketh with himself seven other spirits more wicked than himself, and they enter in and dwell there: and the last state of that man is worse than the first. Even so shall it be also unto this wicked generation (Mt 12:43-45).

There is no analogy here to the Christian. There is no mention of faith or of the presence of the Holy Spirit in the life. There is no reference here to the unregenerate person either. Unfortunately, even Scofield labels this passage "The worthlessness of self-reformation." Such proponents would be pressed to prove that every reforming sinner was once indwelt by a demon.

Actually, Jesus was not referring to a person but to the nation of Israel in His day. He concluded His story with these words, "Even so shall it be also unto this wicked generation." After committing the unpardonable sin, Israel, as personified by her leaders, was now in a far worse spiritual condition that she was before the ministries of Jesus and of John the Baptist. Christ had just announced that there would be no more public signs or miracles to the nation. The next sign would be His coming death and resurrection (Mt 12:38-42). Henceforth, Christ would only be related to the nation on a spiritual basis (Mt 12:46-50). Because of their rejection, Israel would experience judicial blindness and the judgment of God. The nation would be scattered and persecuted until God's program for the church had been completed. In the past, Israel had rejected the messages of the prophets; now, it had spurned the very person of God Himself. Its judgment would be far greater (cf. Mt 11:20-24).

Another misinterpreted passage is found within the con-

text of the Olivet discourse. Jesus said to His disciples,
"But he that shall endure unto the end, the same shall be
saved" (Mt 24:13; cf. Mk 13:13). It is commonly taught
that "the end" refers to the end of one's natural life; therefore, if a person believes and obeys up to his deathbed,
then he will be saved spiritually from hell. However, that
is not the correct meaning of the "end" in this passage.
Jesus had just pointed out the unwillingness of the Jews to
receive Him as their Messiah and their subsequent judgment for doing so (Mt 23:37-38). He then declared, "Ye
shall not see me henceforth, till ye shall say, Blessed is he
that cometh in the name of the Lord" (Mt 23:39). Because of His coming death, resurrection, and ascension
into heaven, Jesus would be both absent from the earth
and unseen by the nation of Israel. However, He would
one day return to the earth, and this time, the Jews would
welcome Him as their King. Jesus then led His disciples out
of the temple into the Mount of Olives. There, the disciples asked Him these searching questions: "Tell us, when
shall these things be? and what shall be the sign of thy
coming, and of the end of the world" (Mt 24:3)? A better
translation of "the end of the world" would be "the end of
the age." When Jesus comes to the earth, the world will
not be destroyed, but it will *end* the time of His absence
from the earth and the period of Israel's rejection of Him.
In this discourse, Jesus is not talking about the end of
someone's life but rather the end of the great tribulation
period. The great tribulation follows the church age and
the rapture of Christians into heaven. Israel will make a
seven-year covenant with the dissembling Antichrist. After
three-and-a-half years, the Antichrist will break the covenant and begin to persecute the Jews terribly. Jesus spoke
about the advent of false Christs and the multiplication
of wars and then added, "See that ye be not troubled:

for all these things must come to pass, but the end is not yet" (Mt 24:6). What "end" was Jesus talking about? Was it not the same "end" mentioned in the disciples' question, the end of the age? Certainly! His coming would also be preceded by famines, pestilences, and earthquakes. Jesus then warned:

> All these are the beginning of sorrows. Then shall they deliver you up to be afflicted, and shall kill you: and ye shall be hated of all nations for my name's sake. And then shall many be offended, and shall betray one another, and shall hate one another. And many false prophets shall rise, and shall deceive many. And because iniquity shall abound, the love of many shall wax cold (Mt 24:8-12).

This passage precedes our problem verse. A person will be saved or delivered from this persecution if he can manage to stay alive until Jesus Christ comes. Christ will destroy the Antichrist and will bring to an end this period of anti-Semitism.

Jesus also said, "And this gospel of the kingdom shall be preached in all the world for a witness unto all nations; and then shall the end come" (Mt 24:14). The same "end" is in view here. How can people argue for perseverance unto the end of one's life (24:13), when this latter verse teaches that the gospel has to be preached throughout the world before the end can come? During the tribulation period, the kingdom message, "Repent ye, for the kingdom of heaven is at hand," will be proclaimed by the dispersed Jews. Once they have done that, Christ will come and will be received by them. The entire Olivet discourse speaks of the end times in Israel's history. There is no reference here to a believer hanging onto God unto the end of his life as a guarantee of his salvation.

Some passages teach the divine chastisement of a Christian even unto physical death, not the possible loss of salvation unto eternal, spiritual death. Chastisement is a mark of sonship. If a professing Christian can sin over and over without being corrected or "spanked" by God, then perhaps he is not a genuine child of the heavenly Father. The author of Hebrews wrote, "But if ye be without chastisement, whereof all are partakers, then are ye bastards, and not sons" (Heb 12:8). There are "illegitimate" children within our churches today; time will reveal their unregenerate condition. Chastisement *must* come to a genuine child of God if he does not confess or forsake his sin. The biblical principle is clear, "For whom the Lord loveth he chasteneth, and scourgeth every son whom he receiveth" (Heb 12:6). There are no exceptions. God chastens His children for their spiritual profit and for the general welfare of the local church. Chastisement takes several forms. It can come in the form of lost privileges, financial setback, material loss, personal illness, and even physical death.

After Paul had full knowledge of the fornication problem in Corinth, he decided "to deliver such an one unto Satan for the destruction of the flesh, that the spirit may be saved in the day of the Lord Jesus" (1 Co 5:5). Note the distinction between the flesh (the body) and the spirit. In spite of the sin of fornication, Paul still regarded the person as a saved man. But what does "destruction of the flesh" have to do with the "deliverance unto Satan"? Later, Paul wrote to Timothy, "Which some having put away concerning faith have made shipwreck: Of whom is Hymenaeus and Alexander; whom I have delivered unto Satan, that they may learn not to blaspheme" (1 Ti 1:19b-20). In both cases, an apostle, namely Paul, determined to take this action. There is no indication that any individual or local church today has this invested authority. This severe discipline seems to be limited to the apostolic era. It was done as a learning experience for the individual and a purging renewal for the church.

Satan was permitted by God to destroy Job's family, wealth, and health; only his life was spared (Job 1-2). Apparently, Peter was delivered unto Satan to learn the evils of pride and the virtues of humility (Lk 22:31). Such a severe chastisement could involve the affliction of the body without death or, possibly, even the inclusion of physical death. In either case, the inner self remained saved. The action was taken for the person's own benefit. It was a corrective, not a punitive, measure.

The carnal Corinthians had also abused the ordinance of the Lord's Table. Some were actually getting drunk in the love feast that preceded the ordinance. Discrimination and selfishness prevailed. After Paul gave the procedure for participation, he warned them,

> Wherefore whosoever shall eat this bread, and drink this cup of the Lord, unworthily, shall be guilty of the body and blood of the Lord. But let a man examine himself, and so let him eat of that bread, and drink of that cup. For he that eateth and drinketh unworthily, eateth and drinketh damnation to himself, not discerning the Lord's body. For this cause many are weak and sickly among you, and many sleep. For if we would judge ourselves, we should not be judged. But when we are judged, we are chastened of the Lord, that we should not be condemned with the world (1 Co 11:27-32).

A better rendering for "damnation" is "judgment." This is not an eternal, punitive judgment (cf. Ro 8:1), but rather a chastening judgment. Many of the Corinthians were afflicted with physical diseases because of their stubborn sins. Others were actually sleeping the sleep of physical death (cf. Jn 11:11-14). God will punish unsaved men for their sins at the great white throne judgment. Since we Christians will not appear there, God must deal with our sins in this present life, and He does, through chastisement. Chastisement can be avoided by the sinning Christian if he confesses and forsakes his sin (cf. 1 Jn 1:9).

However, if he persists, God must take action to stop him. As a loving Father, He spanks lightly at first, but if the child of God does not learn his lesson, then severe chastisement will follow. After all methods fail to bring back the erring child, God may take the Christian home to heaven in premature physical death.

In the conclusion to his book, James wrote,

> Brethren, if any of you do err from the truth, and one convert him; Let him know, that he which converteth the sinner from the error of his way shall save a soul from death, and shall hide a multitude of sins (Ja 5:19-20).

This passage has been misunderstood in two different ways. It has been commonly used for evangelistic motivation to reach the unsaved for Christ. Secondly, some have seen the loss of salvation in these two verses. Both views have missed James' intention. He was speaking to Christians only ("Brethren"). He was referring to the possibility of a Christian brother's disobedience to the Scripture: "If any of you do err from the truth." This is the same person as the sinner mentioned in the next verse. James then admonished the spiritual Christian to minister to his backslidden brother. Paul said the same thing: "Brethren, if a man be overtaken in a fault, ye which are spiritual, restore such an one in the spirit of meekness; considering thyself, lest thou also be tempted" (Gal 6:1). Christians should be concerned when they see their brothers living an unyielded life. They should recognize that persistent sin on the part of a believer will lead to divine chastisement and to loss of effectiveness for the

Christian cause. They should get involved. Jesus taught, "Moreover if thy brother shall trespass against thee, go and tell him his fault between thee and him alone: if he shall hear thee, thou hast gained thy brother" (Mt 18:15). If the sinning Christian repents, then his person ("soul" is used of the total person, both body and soul; cf. 1 Pe 3:20), will be spared premature physical death. Confession of sins brings forgiveness and cleansing (1 Jn 1:9); therefore, a multitude of sins will be hidden.

The "sin unto death" has perplexed many. John wrote,

> If any man see his brother sin a sin which is not unto death, he shall ask, and he shall give him life for them that sin not unto death. There is a sin unto death: I do not say that he shall pray for it. All unrighteousness is sin: and there is a sin not unto death (1 Jn 5:16-17).

What is this "sin unto death"? First of all, it does not refer to a particular sin, but rather to a certain quality of sin. Since the Greek language does not have the indefinite article *a* or *an*, a better translation would be, "There is sin unto death." Second, this type of sin can be committed by a Christian brother. There is no indication that this is a reference to an unsaved person. Spiritual believers should intercede for their sinning brethren, unless the latter are actually sinning that type of sin which will lead to eventual physical death. John implies that there is no hope of rescue for such a person. It is impossible, today, to identify those sins which have the quality of sin unto death. Apparently in the first century, Christians could distinguish between the two types of sin. We simply do not have enough information at our disposal to make a valid judgment today. In any case, this was a type of sin committed by a professing Christian that could lead to the severe chastisement of premature, physical death. There is no indication that eternal death is under discussion here.

Conditional passages have been used as antisecurity arguments. These include clauses introduced by the conditional particle *if*. Some (1 Co 15:1-2; Col 1:23) have been discussed earlier. To the Philippians, Paul wrote,

> That I may know him, and the power of his resurrection, and the fellowship of his sufferings, being made conformable unto his death; If by any means I might attain unto the resurrection of the dead (Phil 3:10-11).

Did Paul doubt that one day he might be excluded from the resurrection? Did he feel that his resurrection depended upon the fulfillment of his announced goals (v. 10)? Certainly not. Paul had already declared that death would be gain for him and that death would usher his soul into the presence of Christ (Phil 1:21-23). Why then did he use *if*? Here is one possibility. Paul wanted to magnify Christ both by life and by death (Phil 1:20). At this time, he was a Roman prisoner. Paul wanted to enter fully into the sufferings of Christ whereby Christ suffered wrongfully at the hands of unjust men. Christ not only suffered, but He died within the will of God by wicked hands. Paul was even willing to submit to such a death. Just as Christ was raised triumphantly from the dead, so Paul desired to share in that victory. The *if* only reflected Paul's belief that Christ could come at any moment and that he would be translated immediately into heaven apart from physical death.

The second possibility is that Paul was talking about a spiritual resurrection. The next few verses reveal his ambition to experience all that God had purposed for him. Paul knew that the same power which raised Jesus Christ from physical death raised him from spiritual death and operated within him so that he might lead a victorious, resurrection life (Eph 1:19–2:6; Ro 6:4). He did not want

to be spiritually insensitive, asleep, or dead (1 Co 15:34).
He wrote these words:

> Always bearing about in the body the dying of the
> Lord Jesus, that the life also of Jesus might be made
> manifest in our body. For we which live are alway de-
> livered unto death for Jesus' sake, that the life also of
> Jesus might be made manifest in our mortal flesh (2 Co
> 4:10-11).

Paul wanted to be dead to self in the will of God so that
he might experience resurrection freshness and newness in
his daily walk. He never doubted his own future, the
translation or the resurrection of his body.

The parables of Jesus have been grossly misinterpreted.
Jesus designed them basically for a Jewish audience both
to reveal and to hide truth (Mt 13:10-17). Even the disciples had trouble understanding their full significance
(Mt 13:36).

In His parable of the sower and the seed (Mt 13:1-23),
Jesus taught that there would be four basic responses to
His ministry, as illustrated by the four different soils:

> When any one heareth the word of the kingdom, and
> understandeth it not, then cometh the wicked one, and
> catcheth away that which was sown in his heart. This is
> he which received seed by the way side. But he that re-
> ceived the seed into stony places, the same is he that
> heareth the word, and anon with joy receiveth it; Yet
> hath he not root in himself, but dureth for a while: for
> when tribulation or persecution ariseth because of the
> word, by and by he is offended. He also that received
> seed among the thorns is he that heareth the word; and
> the care of this world, and the deceitfulness of riches,
> choke the word, and he becometh unfruitful. But he that
> received seed into the good ground is he that heareth the
> word, and understandeth it; which also beareth fruit,

and bringeth forth, some an hundredfold, some sixty, some thirty (Mt 13:19-23).

There are four soils: wayside, stony place, thorny area, and good ground. Some teach that the first three represent people who got saved but who later lost their salvation for various reasons. Only the fourth, the good ground, remained a saved person. But, did Jesus teach that there would be a perfect (100%) response to His ministry or even a fifty percent favorable reception? Hardly! He had said earlier, "Because strait is the gate, and narrow is the way, which leadeth unto life, and few there be that find it" (Mt 7:14). Believers will always be a small minority in the world. Only the good ground speaks of a genuinely saved person. The key words in Christ's explanation are *understanding* and *fruit*. The purpose of sowing seed is to produce fruit, not just a stalk or a blade. The first three did not understand with their heart and therefore failed to experience real conversion (cf. Mt 13:15). The first person (wayside) gave no outward sign of any reception. The second (stony) emotionally reacted to the message without full understanding of the implications of becoming a Christian. Perhaps, he received psychological relief from guilt feelings, but he did not receive spiritual deliverance from moral guilt before a holy God. The third (thorns) was so world-dominated that the seed had no chance. To become a believer, one must fully understand his decision to accept Christ. Such a genuine faith will produce genuine fruit. Some Christians produce more fruit than others, but in all cases, there will be some fruit brought forth.

In the parable of the wheat and the tares (Mt 13:24-30, 36-43), Jesus pointed out the difficulty of distinguishing between saved people (wheat) and unsaved (tares) at times. If men tried to do it, they would fail, because they only observe the exterior. God knows the difference between a wheat and a tare, and in the end of the age, the true nature of people will be revealed. Nowhere is it taught that a wheat stalk can become a tare or that a tare can become wheat. Only those who have always been unsaved (tares) will be cast into hellfire.

The parable of the shut door has caused some confusion and consternation:

> When once the master of the house is risen up, and hath shut to the door, and ye begin to stand without, and to knock at the door, saying, Lord, Lord, open unto us; and he shall answer and say unto you, I know you not whence ye are: Then shall ye begin to say, We have eaten and drunk in thy presence, and thou hast taught in our streets. But he shall say, I tell you, I know you not whence ye are; depart from me, all ye workers of iniquity (Lk 13:25-27).

Jesus was telling the Jewish cities that one day the opportunity to enter into the blessings of the kingdom would be over. Their mere natural association with His person and miraculous ministry would not be sufficient to gain admission. His intimate knowledge of them is the key issue. The Lord knows His own (Jn 10:14; 2 Ti 2:19), and these did not belong to Him. They were, in fact, workers of iniquity (cf. Mt 7:21-23).

The parable of the ungrateful servant (Mt 18:23-35) was given to Peter in response to his question, "Lord, how oft shall my brother sin against me, and I forgive him? till seven times?" (Mt 18:21). Jesus said that "seventy times seven" would be more like it. To explain His answer, Jesus gave the parable. The servant was forgiven a debt of ten thousand talents by his master; however, the servant would not do the same for a fellowservant who owed him only one hundred pence. When the master heard about the ill actions of the ungrateful servant, he "was wroth, and delivered him to the tormentors, till he should pay all that was due unto him" (Mt 18:34). Some have identified God as this lord and a Christian who loses his salvation as the ungrateful servant. Deliverance to the tormentors would be equivalent to expulsion to the lake of fire. One basic principle of hermeneutics is, Don't make a parable walk on all fours. In other words, the parable was designed to teach or to illustrate *one* fundamental spiritual truth; therefore, do not read too much into the various details within the parable. The lord, earlier in the parable, commanded that the servant, his wife, and his children be sold into human slavery (Mt 18:25). Does that sound like the Lord? What does this parable mean, then? Christ ended it with these words: "So likewise shall my heavenly Father do also unto you, if ye from your hearts forgive not every one his brother their trespasses" (Mt 18:35). The basic teaching of this parable is conditional forgiveness: Do not expect God to forgive you of your daily sins if you refuse to forgive others their sins. Your attitude toward your brother's sins manifests your real attitude toward your own sins as you confess them to God. Is your confession a mere ritual or an honest repentance of the heart? In the Sermon on the Mount, Jesus said the same thing:

> Therefore if thou bring thy gift to the altar, and there rememberest that thy brother hath ought against thee; Leave there thy gift before the altar, and go thy way; first be reconciled to thy brother, and then come and offer thy gift (Mt 5:23-24).

God will know whether your desire for forgiveness is genuine by the way in which you treat your brother when he wrongs you.

Jesus used three parables to reveal the attitudes of Israel's religious leaders to Himself and to His message. The parable of the two sons (Mt 21:28-32) contrasted the responses of sinners and of the Pharisees to the revealed will of God. The sinners at first refused to obey, but later repented and did the will of God. The Pharisees said that they would obey but did not support their lip profession with their life. Doing the will of God, not just giving verbal assent to it, is what saves, which is the main idea of this parable.

The second parable, the story of the householder, vineyard, and husbandmen (Mt 21:33-46), revealed how the Pharisees failed to discharge their responsibility in their spiritual care of Israel. They (husbandmen) mistreated God's servants and actually killed the householder's son (Jesus Christ). They refused to turn over to Christ and to God what rightfully belonged to Them. Matthew wrote, "And when the chief priests and Pharisees had heard his parables, they perceived that he spake of them" (Mt 21:45). Jesus said that the householder would miserably destroy the wicked husbandmen. It cannot be argued that these husbandmen lost their salvation. Who would argue that the priests and Pharisees were ever saved? Because of their sin and unbelief, these religious leaders would forever forfeit their position of spiritual responsibility.

The parable of the marriage feast (Mt 22:1-14) showed how the Pharisees rejected the offer to participate in the blessings of the marriage feast (marriage between the Messiah and the believing remnant of Israel). Because of their rejection, both they and their city would be destroyed. The Romans accomplished this in A.D. 70. The spiritual blessings were then extended to the unworthy Gentiles and Jewish sinners who were clothed in the righteousness of Christ. The man without a wedding garment was an unsaved Pharisee who tried to get into the banquet after earlier refusing the offer.

In none of the preceding three parables is there any indication that Jesus was talking about the loss of salvation by genuine believers. Only the unsaved religious leaders of Israel are within the scope of these parables.

In the Olivet discourse, Jesus was outlining for His disciples the course of world events prior to His second advent to the earth. Within the discourse, He addressed that generation of Jews that would be living during the great tribulation period (cf. Mt 24:15, "When *ye* therefore shall see"). Since no one on earth will know the exact time of His coming (Mt 24:36), it will be necessary to be prepared for the unexpected.

Jesus equated the period of His second advent with the time of Noah (Mt 24:37-41). In that preflood era, only Noah was ready, prepared, and watching. The unsaved went their merry way, totally indifferent to the message of Noah and to the coming judgment. Jesus then gave three parables to illustrate the proper attitudes that people should have in the great tribulation prior to His second coming. They should be like the faithful and wise servant who was doing the master's will with the full knowledge that the master could return to the house at any moment (Mt 24:45-51). The unsaved are like the evil servant who got drunk and smote God's faithful servants. They compare to the unsaved of Noah's day, who will be judged for their sin.

In the parable of the ten virgins (Mt 25:1-13), the saved Jews of the tribulation will be like the five wise virgins who were watching and who were fully prepared to meet the bridegroom (Christ). The unsaved are equated to the five foolish virgins who were not prepared. To them, the bridegroom later said, "Verily I say unto you, I know you not" (Mt 25:12). Some have argued that the oil in the lamps represents the Holy Spirit; however, the believer does not carry the Spirit around in a vessel; He indwells the life. This oil could be bought with money; can the Spirit of God be purchased?

The parable of the servants and the talents revealed the faithful discharge of responsibility as over against the failure of the wicked and slothful servant (Mt 25:14-30). This latter servant is the same type as the wicked husbandmen who refused to surrender the fruits of the vineyard to the master. He was afraid of his lord's coming; the believer looks forward to that great event. In the great tribulation, the true Jewish believer will be waiting, watching, and working. He will be fully prepared, as Noah, for the coming of his Lord.

Another group of problem passages deals with warnings to professing believers. The various exhortations and warnings found within the book of Hebrews serve as excellent examples of this type. The entire book was written to show the superiority of a person's position in Christ to that which a person had before God under the law. The author demonstrated that Christ was better than the prophets (1:1-3), the angels (1:4—2:18), Moses (3:1—4:13), and the Levitical priesthood (4:14—10:18). Christ's priesthood was better than the Old Testament or the existing Judaistic priesthood in position, in order, in covenant basis, in type of sanctuary served, and in the type of sacrifice offered. Why was the author showing this type of superiority? Because the professing Jewish Christians were thinking about returning to the worship of God within the existing temple, to the sacrifice system in order to avoid future persecution by fellow Jews and to display their national identity with Israel in the face of Roman threats.

The author of Hebrews regarded his readers as professing believers. He called them "brethren" (3:1, 12) and "beloved" (6:9). Although they had been saved for some time, they were immature in the faith (5:11-14). They had joyfully suffered persecution before, but now they were growing weary of it. The book, then, was written to encourage them to go on with the Lord. The author wanted to stir them on to a life of patient endurance and faith, as they anticipated the coming of the Lord and the destruction of Jerusalem and the temple (10:25, 37). To do so, the author incorporated warnings. To go on meant blessing; to go back would avoid persecution, but it would also bring divine chastisement. Chastisement at the hand of God should be feared more than persecution by man.

Here is his first warning:

> For if the word spoken by angels was stedfast, and every transgression and disobedience received a just recompence of reward; How shall we escape, if we neglect so great salvation; which at the first began to be spoken by the Lord, and was confirmed unto us by them that heard him (Heb 2:2-3).

Angels had a part in the giving of the Mosaic law to Israel (Gal 3:19). Whenever a Jew broke the law, he suffered the penalty for that violation. If some professing Christian disobeys what Christ has spoken (and He is greater than the angels), he will not escape the penalty or chastisement either.

Later, the author wrote,

> Take heed, brethren, lest there be in any of you an evil heart of unbelief, in departing from the living God. But exhort one another daily, while it is called To day; lest any of you be hardened through the deceitfulness of sin (Heb 3:12-13).

The experience of these Jewish Christians was equated to the wilderness wanderings of Israel under the direction of Moses. The people, redeemed out of Egyptian bondage, had been led by God through the parted waters of the Red

Sea, on to Sinai where they received the law, and had finally arrived at Kadesh-barnea, the southern entrance to Canaan. God and Moses told them to enter the land and to claim the blessings within the land promised to their fathers (Abraham, Isaac, and Jacob); however, the people refused to enter. They were afraid of possible death at the hands of the giants and of other inhabitants within the country. They did not believe that the God who had redeemed them and who had led them this far could give them victory over future conflicts. Because of that unbelief, that generation of Israelites was punished with forty years of wandering in the wilderness.

According to the author of Hebrews, these Christians had come to a spiritual Kadesh-barnea. Would they continue to trust God for daily direction and provision, or would they doubt? The author, like Joshua and Caleb of old, wanted to encourage the people to go with Christ in spite of future persecutions. If they tried to avoid the conflict, they would only fall back into the chastising hands of God.

He added, "For we are made partakers of Christ, if we hold the beginning of our confidence stedfast unto the end" (Heb 3:14). In what sense are we made partakers of Christ? The author was not talking about initial salvation, but rather, the daily fullness of the Christian life, which is only possible through total obedience to the will of God. The generation of Moses never experienced the daily material and spiritual blessings that God had provided, because of their unbelief; the author does not want his readers to make the same mistake.

Probably the most controversial passage within Hebrews is this:

> For it is impossible for those who were once enlightened, and have tasted of the heavenly gift, and were

> made partakers of the Holy Ghost, And have tasted the
> good word of God, and the powers of the world to come,
> If they shall fall away, to renew them again unto re-
> pentance; seeing they crucify to themselves the Son of
> God afresh, and put him to an open shame (Heb 6:4-6)

Who are these people? Are they saved or unsaved? Scofield regards them as professing believers who fall short of
genuine faith after coming to the very threshold of salvation. But examine the description of these people. As
blinded sinners, they were enlightened in that God shined
in their hearts "to give the light of the knowledge of the
glory of God in the face of Jesus Christ" (2 Co 4:6). They
tasted the heavenly gift to the same degree that Christ
"tasted" death for every man (Heb 2:9). Jesus did not
sample the cup of divine wrath; He drank it all down. Believers drink of the Holy Spirit and are indwelt by Him
(Ro 8:9; 1 Co 12:13). These are definitely saved individuals. How then can they fall away? First of all, the
phrase, "if they shall fall away," is actually a translation of
a single Greek participle, not of a conditional clause. This
may or may not be a conditional participle. The author
may be describing an actual occurrence, and not just a
hypothetical possibility (or impossibility as some think).

Remember the background of this epistle and of this
passage. These Jewish believers were at a crossroads.
Should they go on with Christ in daily living with the full
knowledge that persecution was inevitable, or should they
retreat? At Kadesh-barnea, the Israelites doubted or fell
away; they decided not to go on into the land. After their
punishment was declared to them, they then decided to
reverse their original decision, but it was too late (Num
14). They could not be renewed to repentance. The author was warning his readers that they could not withdraw
to the safety of worship within Judaism until the heat of

persecution was past and then realign themselves with the Christians and take up where they had left off. This was impossible. Their situation may be a fitting example of "sin unto death." As long as they brought forth spiritual fruit, things that accompany salvation including a labor of love toward fellow believers, God would continue to work with them. But, whenever the time should come that they would thoroughly quench the fruit-producing work of the Spirit, then God would have to chastise them as He did Israel. They could lose their lives in premature death even as the Israelites in the wilderness.

A passing observation is appropriate here. If this passage taught that a Christian could lose his salvation, as some identify "falling away," does it also teach that he can get it back? The typical Arminian approach is that a Christian can regain lost salvation through renewed faith. But, the author said that it was impossible to renew fallen ones to repentance. If this passage were teaching the loss of salvation, it would also be warning that it could not be regained. There would be no comfort to the Arminian here.

A similar warning is given later in the book:

> For if we sin willfully after that we have received the knowledge of the truth, there remaineth no more sacrifice for sins, But a certain fearful looking for of judgment and fiery indignation, which shall devour the adversaries (Heb 10:26-27).

The author had given "the knowledge of the truth" to his readers in the first ten chapters: they have a *better* position in Christ. Under the law there was no animal sacrifice that could be offered for presumptuous or willful sin. Since there was no way back to God, the person would receive capital punishment. The situation of these Jewish

Christians was similar. If they defected from the Christian assembly to temple worship, there was no way back; they, too, would be chastised severely.

The author ends his argument with this comparison:

> Lest there be any fornicator, or profane person, as Esau, who for one morsel of meat sold his birthright. For ye know how that afterward, when he would have inherited the blessing, he was rejected: for he found no place of repentance, though he sought it carefully with tears (Heb 12:16-17).

For one moment of physical relief, Esau sold his spiritual privileges. He did not lose his salvation because he sold his birthright; he lost the daily blessing of family spiritual leadership. Later, when he wanted it, he could not get it back. His decision was similar to that of the Israelites at Kadesh. There was no possible reversal of his action.

The last book of the Bible ends with an awesome warning:

> For I testify unto every man that heareth the words of the prophecy of this book, If any man shall add unto these things, God shall add unto him the plagues that are written in this book: And if any man shall take away from the words of the book of this prophecy, God shall take away his part out of the book of life, and out of the holy city, and from the things which are written in this book (Rev 22:18-19).

This warning applies not only to the book of Revelation (primary meaning), but also to the entire revealed Word of God (secondary application). God progressively revealed His written Word to man; this warning demonstrates that His written revelation had come to a close. Nothing could be added to it or subtracted from it. This warning therefore does not apply to the sins of adultery, theft, or backsliding. Would any genuine believer ever add to or take away from the revealed truth of the Bible? Certainly not. It stands as a hypothetical possibility, but also as a practical impossibility. It is similar to Paul's warning: "But though [if] we, or an angel from heaven, preach any other gospel unto you than that which we have preached unto you, let him be accursed" (Gal 1:8). *Could* Paul do it? Yes. *Would* he do it? No. Only the unsaved founders of sects and the arrogant higher critics would dare to tamper with God's Word.

This was a double-sided warning. For addition, God would add these plagues. This was basically a physical judgment. But how could God add the plagues of the great tribulation (Rev 6-16) to a person who has lived and died within the church age? It could only be possible to the unsaved person living at the time of the rapture of the church. In that case, he would enter the tribulation and be exposed to these plagues. For subtraction, God would remove a man's part from the book of life. (Most Greek texts read this as the "tree of life.") Again, if this person was living at the end of the church age, he would lose his life during the tribulation and would not be able to enter into the millennial kingdom or into the holy city, which may be on earth during Christ's earthly reign.

The "book of life" has intrigued many. Those "whose names are not written in the book of life of the Lamb slain from the foundation of the world" (Rev 13:8) will worship the anti-Christ as God during the great tribulation. Such people will be amazed as they witness the rise of the anti-Christ to power (Rev 17:8). Only those who "are written in the Lamb's book of life" will enter the holy city (Rev 21:27). At the great white throne judgment, "whosoever was not found written in the book of life was cast into the lake of fire" (Rev 20:15). The question is obvious: can the name of a Christian ever be blotted out of the book of life, thus causing the loss of his salvation?

What is the book of life? First, it does seem to contain a roster of the names of saved people. When the disciples returned rejoicing over the results of their preaching and healing, Jesus said, "Notwithstanding in this rejoice not, that the spirits are subject unto you; but rather rejoice, because your names are written in heaven" (Lk 10:20). In what are they written? Probably, the Lamb's book of life. Paul remarked that the names of his fellowlaborers were in the book of life (Phil 4:3).

However, there is a second sense in which the book of life contains a list of names of those who are presently alive on earth. It would therefore be a book of *physical* life. David wrote concerning his enemies, "Let them be blotted out of the book of the living, and not be written with the righteous" (Ps 69:28). He was asking for physical vengeance. The psalm nowhere implies that his enemies were saved spiritually; contrariwise, David wanted them to lose their natural lives because of their mistreatment of him, the earthly representative and ruler of God. Their enmity against David was really enmity against God.

When Israel sinned in the worship of the golden calf, Moses interceded before God in their behalf:

> Yet now, if thou wilt forgive their sin—; and if not, blot me, I pray thee, out of thy book which thou hast written. And the LORD said unto Moses, Whosoever hath sinned against me, him will I blot out of my book (Ex 32:32-33).

Moses may have been voicing an impossible request. Paul wished that He could spend an eternity in the lake of fire if the entire nation of Israel could be saved (Ro 9:3), but that could never be granted. However, Moses may have been offering himself as a physical substitute for the nation. If there was to be no forgiveness for the breaking of the first commandment, then Moses wanted to die vicariously. The nation was spared, but the involved individuals died in the plague that God sent. Again, physical death is the essence of being blotted out of the book of life.

To the church of Sardis, Jesus admonished, "He that overcometh, the same shall be clothed in white raiment; and I will not blot out his name out of the book of life, but I will confess his name before my Father, and before his angels" (Rev 3:5). This is really a promise to the overcomer, not a warning. The overcomer is the genuine believer. Three pledges are given to him, including a negative and a positive description of salvation. This is similar to Christ's promise: "He that heareth my word, and believeth on him that sent me, hath everlasting life, and shall not come into condemnation; but is passed from death unto life" (Jn 5:24). The promise to the overcomer contains a positive truth, not the negative inference of a threat. It is like a Christian giving testimony, "Because I am saved, I will not go to hell, but I will go to heaven."

The final group of problem passages concerns the lives of certain biblical characters. In real life, the discussion over eternal security often boils down to personalities rather than to principles. Too often, doctrines are developed by exegeting people instead of Scripture. Typical questions as these are asked: "How could Dick be a genuine Christian and commit adultery?" Or, "How can Jane call herself a believer and yet spend most of her time with unsaved people?" It would be impossible to evaluate each particular situation; one would have to be both omnipresent and omniscient.

It is possible, however, to evaluate the lives of some of the biblical characters. These were real people with real problems. Let us look at them and try to determine their spiritual condition.

Lot was an enigma. He journeyed with Abraham from Ur to Haran and on to Canaan. Lot prospered materially through his association with his uncle (Gen 13:5). Lot made an economically wise but spiritually poor choice when he decided to move his flocks to the Jordan plain near Sodom and Gomorrah. The people of Sodom were exceedingly wicked sinners (Gen 13:13). Even the intercession of Abraham could not save the city from divine judgment. Lot tried to protect the angelic visitors, and yet he was willing to surrender his daughters for sexual abuse to the men of Sodom (Gen 19:1-8). He had no moral influence over his sons-in-law, and possibly little over his wife. The end of his life was tragically marked by his intimate sexual relationships with his own daughters (although unknown to him *because of his drunkenness*).

Could a person like Lot be saved? Remember that Abraham prayed for him. The spiritual condition of Lot may be implied in Abraham's question, "Wilt thou also destroy the righteous with the wicked?" (Gen 18:23). Remember that God sent angels to his house to drag him out of the city. Peter gives the clearest answer:

> And turning the cities of Sodom and Gomorrha into ashes condemned them with an overthrow, making them an ensample unto those that after should live ungodly; And delivered just Lot, vexed with the filthy conversation of the wicked. (For that righteous man dwelling among them, in seeing and hearing, vexed his righteous soul from day to day with their unlawful deeds;) The Lord knoweth how to deliver the godly out of temptations, and to reserve the unjust unto the day of judgment to be punished (2 Pe 2:6-9).

Just Lot! Peter calls him just, righteous (twice), and,

indirectly, godly. Only a believer could be vexed in the inner man as Lot was. Lot lost all that he had because of his close personal relationship to Sodom, but he was positionally righteous. Today, we wonder how a believer could live in the midst of such moral filth. Lot did, and he was affected by it. His inner man suffered, and that is how any genuine believer would respond to that type of environment. Lot had no testimony, but he was still saved. He is probably a good example of an immature, carnal believer.

Could anyone question the spiritual condition of Abraham, the "Friend of God?" (Ja 2:23). Throughout the Old Testament, God revealed Himself to Israel as the God of Abraham, Isaac, and Jacob (Ex 3:6). God established Abraham as the father of the Messianic nation through the many unconditional promises given in the Abrahamic covenant (Gen 12:1-3; 13:14-18; 15:18-21; 17:1-8). The first mention of the act of faith which secures divine righteousness is associated with Abraham (Gen 15:6). In fact, Abraham is recognized and recommended to the Christian as a prime example of the man of faith (Ro 4:1-5; Gal 3:6-9; Heb 11:8-19). Spiritually speaking, when a sinner is born into the family of God, he also becomes a child of Abraham (Gal 3:29).

It would appear to the casual reader that Abraham was perfect; yet, he too had his moral flaws. Shortly after he entered Canaan, Abraham showed a lack of faith in God's material provision by going to Egypt to escape the effects of famine. There he lied, passing his wife, Sarah, off as his sister to avoid possible physical harm or death to himself (Gen 12:10-20). In fact, he repeated this same sin of misrepresentation later before Abimelech in Gerar (Gen 20). God had promised Abraham and Sarah a child, but no child came for twelve years. Out of desperation and a lack of patience, Abraham listened to Sarah (instead of to God) and had an intimate relationship with Hagar, Sarah's domestic servant. This must be regarded as sexual sin; yet, God did not withdraw His promise; Isaac was born thirteen years later. When the entire life of Abraham is evaluated, he must be seen as a mature, spiritual believer who had moments of carnal expression.

Samson was another paradox. His extraordinary zeal for God was completely offset by his love for Philistine women. He was a Nazarite from his mother's womb and served as a judge over Israel for twenty years (Judg 13:5; 15:20). When the Spirit of the Lord came upon him, he was endued with unusual physical strength. He could kill a young lion or thirty Philistines with his bare hands, or a thousand men with the jawbone of an ass. No bond could hold him while he was under the control of the Holy Spirit. After Samson's famous hair was cut, he became impotent. Unaware of this, he said, "I will go out as at other times before, and shake myself. And he [knew] not that the LORD was departed from him" (Judg 16:20). How was the Lord departed from him? Some would say that Samson lost his salvation because he revealed his secret to Delilah. However, there is no mention of that possibility in this context.

In the Old Testament period, the Holy Spirit came upon a believer so that the latter could perform an unusual task for God. He came upon the craftsmen so that they might construct the tabernacle according to God's specifications (Ex 31:2-5). He came upon Gideon so that he might lead the Israelites to military victory over the Midianites (Judg 6:34).

Just as the Spirit sovereignly came upon a person, so He could leave at will. When He did, the person was then incapable of doing what he had previously done under the enablement of the Spirit. The coming and going of the Spirit in the pre-Calvary period should not be identified or confused with the gaining and losing of one's salvation.

Because of Samson's disobedience, the Spirit left Samson. The unusual physical enablement was likewise removed. Samson did not know this, and thus he was captured and blinded by the Philistines. Later, in the house of Dagon, Samson prayed, "O Lord God, remember me, I pray thee, and strengthen me, I pray thee, only this once, O God, that I may be at once avenged of the Philistines for my two eyes" (Judg 16:28). He did not pray for the restoration of his salvation; he had never lost it. Rather, he prayed for the return of unusual physical strength. God answered that prayer, and Samson pushed aside the support pillars. Samson is listed in the "hall of faith" (Heb 11:32). Throughout his life he was marked by a firm allegiance to the God of Israel. He believed in God and in His enablement, although he often disobeyed His written precepts.

Many have wondered about Saul, the first king of Israel. Was he saved or unsaved? If he was a believer, how could he want to kill David? How can his behavior be explained? Saul brought some excellent qualities to the kingship (1 Sa 9). He was a choice young man, goodly, physically impressive, obedient to his father, respectful of men of God, and humble. When Samuel anointed Saul with oil, the former said, "Is it not because the LORD hath anointed thee to be captain over his inheritance" (1 Sa 10:1)? Would God appoint Samuel to anoint an unsaved man over Israel? Certainly not! Later, Israel did have wicked kings, but they ruled in succession of their fathers, not by direct appointment. Samuel also said to Saul, "And the Spirit of the LORD will come upon thee, and thou shalt prophesy with [the prophets], and shalt be turned into another man"

(1 Sa 10:6). Does the Spirit of the Lord come upon un-saved people? Hardly! God gave Saul another heart (1 Sa 10:9). Saul was later accompanied by "a band of men, whose hearts God had touched" (1 Sa 10:26). Would such people have identified themselves with an unregenerate, royal aspirant?

In his emotional and spiritual immaturity, Saul made three errors of judgment in the early years of his reign. In his impatience, he presumed to offer a sacrifice to God in the absence of a priest (1 Sa 13:8-12). He imposed a terrible prohibition of food upon his armies and even planned to kill Jonathan, his son, because, not knowing the decree, he ate food (1 Sa 14). He failed to kill all of the Amalekites and their flocks (1 Sa 15). His punishment for this triple error was severe. Samuel announced to him, "Because thou hast rejected the word of the LORD, he hath also rejected thee from being king" (1 Sa 15:23).

Samuel was then instructed by God to anoint David to be the next king. When this occurred, "The Spirit of the LORD came upon David from that day forward" (1 Sa 16:13). David would now experience the divine work of preparation and enablement for his new task of ruling Israel.

What happened to Saul? The writer observed, "But the Spirit of the LORD departed from Saul, and an evil spirit from the LORD troubled him" (1 Sa 16:14). Did Saul lose his salvation? No! His usefulness was now over; he was put on the shelf. He no longer had divine enablement for the task. In fact, depression and paranoia seemed to possess him (perhaps the meaning of the "evil spirit from the LORD").

Saul could not face the fact that he had been rejected by God. His resistance to the revealed will of God caused him to take out his antagonism upon God's anointed, David

(1 Sa 16:14–27:12). Unable to slay David, he feared for his own life, especially in conflicts with the Philistines. In desperation, he even consulted a witch about the outcome of a future battle (1 Sa 28). He later died in that battle (1 Sa 31). In his lamentation over the deaths of his friends, David sang:

> Saul and Jonathan were lovely and pleasant in their lives, and in their death they were not divided: they were swifter than eagles, they were stronger than lions. Ye daughters of Israel, weep over Saul, who clothed you in scarlet, with other delights, who put on ornaments of gold upon your apparel (2 Sa 1:23-24).

This funeral eulogy reveals that David regarded them as believers. Saul was just a good example of a child of God who was both carnal and immature. His active resistance to the will of God caused him anxiety and possible temporary insanity. It perhaps was his sin unto death. He lost his life prematurely because he would not conform to the revealed will of the Lord.

What a beautiful life the shepherd-king David lived. He returned Saul's hatred with love. He overcame civil war to become the king. He defeated the enemies of Israel and secured the nation's borders. He established Jerusalem as the religious and political center of his empire. He longed to build a temple for God out of his love and gratitude toward Him, but it was not within the divine will. His psalms reveal his intimate fellowship with God. And yet, at the very height of his life, he committed that infamous sin of adultery with Bathsheba (2 Sa 11). How could he do it? He was in the wrong place at the wrong time. He saw her, inquired about her, sent for her, took her, and lay with her. David had a sin nature, and for that short period, yielded to its desires:

> But every man is tempted, when he is drawn away of
> his own lust, and enticed. Then when lust hath con-
> ceived, it bringeth forth sin: and sin, when it is finished,
> bringeth forth death (Ja 1:14-15).

Bathsheba became pregnant, and David became fright-
ened. After failing to disguise his sin, David arranged for
the death of Uriah, Bathsheba's husband, at the battle-
front. David had indeed broken several of the Ten Commandments.

When Nathan the prophet told David about a rich man
who stole the only lamb of a poor man, David replied,
"As the LORD liveth, the man that hath done this thing
shall surely die: And he shall restore the lamb fourfold,
because he did this thing, and because he had no pity" (2
Sa 12:5-6). Then, Nathan revealed that David *was* the
man. Touched and convicted, David confessed his sin
(2 Sa 12:13). Psalm 51 reveals the inner agony that per-
meated David's soul at this time:

> Make me to hear joy and gladness; that the bones which
> thou hast broken may rejoice.
> Hide thy face from my sins, and blot out all mine
> iniquities.
> Create in me a clean heart, O God; and renew a right
> spirit within me.
> Cast me not away from thy presence; and take not thy
> holy spirit from me.
> Restore unto me the joy of thy salvation; and uphold
> me with thy free spirit (Ps 51:8-12).

David did not want to be rejected from his kingship as
Saul had been. If the enabling Spirit would leave him,
David would be through. David was a broken man; he
knew the greatness of his sin. He asked that God restore
unto him the *joy* of his salvation. David did not forfeit his
salvation with his adultery, but he did lose the joy. With

hidden, unconfessed sin in his life, how could he enjoy God? David deserved to die for his sin, but God graciously spared him. However, chastisement was still in order. David lost four sons (the infant son of Bathsheba, Amnon, Absalom, and Adonijah) because he took the life of Uriah. His family and kingdom were never the same after that episode. David was a type of the mature, spiritual believer who paid a terrible price in this life for one moment of carnal satisfaction. When his entire life is put into proper perspective, it still must be said that David was a man after God's own heart.

The New Testament also has some problem characters. What about Judas? Could he be an apostle and yet not be saved? Did he lose his salvation by his act of betrayal? It was within the divine will that the selection of the twelve apostles from the many disciples would include a materially minded, unsaved person who would provide the means of arrest. Jesus said, "Have not I chosen you twelve, and one of you is a devil? He spake of Judas Iscariot the son of Simon: for he it was that should betray him, being one of the twelve" (Jn 6:70-71). Judas may have been the treasurer of the apostolic band. If so, he had stolen from the money bag. That is why he was so upset over the "waste" of the expensive ointment poured over Christ's feet (Jn 12:1-6). He probably wanted to replenish what he had stolen before he was found out.

When Jesus announced His betrayal to His disciples, no one suspected Judas. His true spiritual nature was not obvious to other men, but Jesus knew his heart. At the washing of the disciples' feet, Jesus said,

> He that is washed needeth not save to wash his feet, but is clean every whit: and ye are clean, but not all. For he knew who should betray him; therefore said he, ye are not all clean (Jn 13:10-11).

Judas had never experienced the complete washing of regeneration (Titus 3:5). He knew it, and so did Jesus. At the supper table, Satan entered into the body of Judas (Jn 13:27). Nowhere in the Scripture is it taught that a *believer* can be indwelt by Satan or a fallen angel.

Jesus called Judas "the son of perdition" (Jn 17:12). This title is used elsewhere only of the anti-Christ (2 Th 2:3), and no one would argue for that person's salvation. In fact, because of this double usage, some have argued that the anti-Christ will be Judas, raised from the dead.

The "repentance" of Judas has caused some perplexity. Matthew wrote,

> Then Judas, which had betrayed him, when he saw that he was condemned, repented himself and brought again the thirty pieces of silver to the chief priests and elders, Saying, I have sinned in that I have betrayed the innocent blood. And they said, what is that to us? see thou to that. And he cast down the pieces of silver in the temple, and departed, and went and hanged himself (Mt 27:3-5).

What kind of repentance was this? This particular Greek word indicates an emotional regret (*metamelomai*), not a repentance of moral and spiritual guilt (*metanoeo*). Judas was sorry over what had happened to Jesus because he did not realize that it would go that far. After being with Jesus three years, he knew that Jesus was not worthy of death. He tried to reverse the trial action by returning the money, but it was too late. In remorse, he hanged himself. If this had been genuine repentance, he would have sought out Jesus or the eleven apostles.

When the disciples prayed about the appointment of the twelfth apostle, they said,

> Thou, Lord, which knowest the hearts of all men, shew whether of these two thou hast chosen, That he may take

part of this ministry and apostleship, from which Judas by transgression fell, that he might go to his own place (Ac 1:24-25).

Judas did not fall from salvation; he fell from the apostleship. There is a vast difference. Judas is a perfect example of those unsaved Christian workers mentioned by Jesus in the conclusion of the Sermon on the Mount:

> Not every one that saith unto me, Lord, Lord, shall enter into the kingdom of heaven; but he that doeth the will of my Father which is in heaven. Many will say to me in that day, Lord, Lord, have we not prophesied in thy name? and in thy name have cast out devils? and in thy name done many wonderful works? And then will I profess unto them, I never knew you: depart from me, ye that work iniquity (Mt 7:21-23).

Judas had done all of these things (Mt 10; Lk 10). He had performed a ministry for Christ, but he did not know Christ as his Saviour from sin. He was a totally unsaved man, from the beginning to the end.

In the revival at Samaria, a sorcerer, Simon, was attracted to the gospel by Philip's miracles (Ac 8:5-12). Luke wrote, "Then Simon himself believed also: and when he was baptized, he continued with Philip, and wondered, beholding the miracles and signs which were done" (Ac 8:13). Later, when Peter and John imparted the Holy Spirit to the converts through their prayer and laying on of hands, Simon made a request of the two apostles, offering them money:

> Saying, Give me also this power, that on whomsoever I lay hands, he may receive the Holy Ghost. But Peter said unto him, Thy money perish with thee, because thou hast thought that the gift of God may be purchased with money. Thou hast neither part nor lot in this matter: for thy heart

is not right in the sight of God. Repent therefore of this thy wickedness, and pray God, if perhaps the thought of thine heart may be forgiven thee. For I perceive that thou art in the gall of bitterness, and in the bond of iniquity. Then answered Simon, and said, Pray ye to the Lord for me, that none of these things which ye have spoken come upon me (Ac 8:19-24).

From this account, the question is obvious: was Simon really saved? It is difficult to make a dogmatic judgment here. There are two strong possible solutions however.

The first is that Simon really was saved, but in his immaturity and carnality, he reflected the desires of his unsaved days in his request. New converts *do* bring into their Christian experience bad habits, false concepts, and prejudices. They have to be instructed in order to know what is proper spiritual thinking and living. Simon loved power and prestige when he was practicing his sorcery (Ac 8:9-11). When he saw the apostolic power of Peter and John, he naturally (from his sin nature) desired it. He thought that spiritual greatness could be purchased. Remember that the disciples also once asked Christ for positions of authority. Through the washing of their feet, Jesus told them that the essence of spiritual greatness was humility and service to others. Luke does say that Simon believed and was baptized. If that verse is taken at face value, then Simon must have been saved. When Peter criticized Simon, he told the former sorcerer to repent and to pray. Simon responded by asking for their intercession. Did Peter tell Simon to get saved, or to repent as a believer in order to escape the chastisement of physical death? The second choice would be consistent with the passage. The case study of Simon was therefore included in Acts as a warning that only apostles had this invested authority and that spiritual greatness is not achieved through selfish ambition.

A second possible interpretation of this passage is that Simon really was not saved. Simon loved self-exaltation:

> But there was a certain man, called Simon, which beforetime in the same city used sorcery, and bewitched the people of Samaria, giving out that himself was some great one: To whom they all gave heed, from the least to the greatest, saying, This man is the great power of God. And to him they had regard, because that of long time he had bewitched them with sorceries (Ac 8:9-11).

When the Samaritans accepted Christ through Philip's preaching and miracles, Simon saw that his influence was declining and that Philip had taken his place. In fact, Philip did things that Simon thought to be impossible. Simon believed, but *what* did he believe? He believed that Philip had unusual power. His situation would be no different than those Jews who believed that Jesus was a miracle worker and a divinely sent teacher but who never really committed themselves to Him in saving faith (Jn 6). His lust for this power became evident in his request. Peter treated him as an unsaved person, and he responded with fear, not faith. This event was included by Luke to show that unsaved men could fake genuine belief in order to gain entrance into the church.

Both of the preceding interpretations are possible within the context. Not enough information is given to make a firm conclusion. Because of this fact, no one should argue from this passage that salvation can be lost.

We have looked at many problem passages in this chapter; however, all of the problems can be resolved and harmonized with the clear teaching of eternal security elsewhere. The Bible does not teach two opposite doctrines; its theology is consistent throughout.

6

What Is Your Spiritual Condition?

PEOPLE HAVE BEEN CLASSIFIED in different ways. There are the two sexes. One can belong to one of several race groups: black, white, red, or yellow. Economically, one is either poor, rich, or middle class. Nationalities are multiple.

As far as God is concerned, there are only two major categories of men: the unsaved and the saved. This is where human misunderstanding manifests itself. Many do not know what a genuine Christian is. Too often, they confuse the practice of a believer with his position. Some expect a child of God to be absolutely perfect one day, one week, or one month after his conversion.

No one expects a newborn infant to act like an adult. Young people, through adolescence and the teen years, should be afforded the luxury of making mistakes. So it is with the Christian. As a child of God grows and matures from spiritual infancy to adulthood, he should receive compassion and direction from older Christians, not criticism, whenever he sins or makes an error of judgment.

The Scriptures identify these different relationships or conditions people have before God.

First, man sustains a certain relationship to the Spirit of God and to spiritual truth. When Paul wrote to the Corinthians, he proposed several guidelines that form the background of this discussion (1 Co 2:9–3:4). Natural man, in himself, would never imagine the content of divine, spiritual truth: "But as it is written, Eye hath not seen, nor ear heard, neither have entered into the heart of man, the things which God hath prepared for them" (2:9). Spiritual truth has been revealed by God to man through the Spirit in the written Word of God: "But God hath revealed them unto us by his Spirit" (2:10a). Only the Spirit knows the content of the divine mind:

> For the Spirit searcheth all things, yea, the deep things of God. For what man knoweth the things of a man, save the spirit of man which is in him? even so the things of God knoweth no man, but the Spirit of God (2:10b-11).

Every Christian is indwelt by the Holy Spirit. "Now we have received, not the spirit of the world, but the spirit which is of God" (2:12a). Every believer is now in a position to be taught spiritual truth: "that we might know the things that are freely given to us of God " (2:12b). The words of the human, biblical authors are actually the divine words of God. They are not man-originated, but Spirit-given. "Which things also we speak, not in the words which man's wisdom teacheth, but which the Holy Ghost teacheth" (2:13a). The spiritual truth of the Bible can only be known through proper interpretation and application under the direction of the Spirit: "comparing spiritual things with spiritual" (2:13b). At this point, Paul then began to describe three kinds of men who bear three different relationships to the Spirit of God and to spiritual truth.

The first type of man is the natural man. He is a "soulish" (*psuchikos*, Greek) person. He is unsaved and fits totally within the description of the unregenerate man. Because the Spirit of God does not indwell him, he does not have the capacity to receive spiritual truth. Paul wrote, "But the natural man receiveth not the things of the Spirit of God: for they are foolishness unto him: neither can he know them, because they are spiritually discerned" (2:14).

Imagine that the natural man is like an AM-FM radio. God is transmitting spiritual truth by way of the Heavenly Broadcasting System (HBS) on an FM frequency. The FM part of the natural man's receiver is totally broken; only the AM works, and it is tuned into the World Broadcasting System (WBS). This man has no capacity to receive the divine transmission of truth. His real need is a total repair job of the FM works. In a sense, this is what happens when regeneration takes place. The believing sinner receives a new nature, thus giving him the capacity for the first time to receive spiritual truth.

The second type of man is the spiritual man. He is a saved man who not only possesses the indwelling presence of the Holy Spirit but who also is totally yielded to Him. He thus is in a position to discern the will of God and to ascertain spiritual truth: "But he that is spiritual judgeth all things, yet he himself is judged of no man" (2:15). His mind and heart are focused on Christ: "For who hath known the mind of the Lord, that he may instruct him? But we have the mind of Christ" (2:16). Any Christian can be spiritual if he wants to be. Spirituality is not based upon the length of time one has been a Christian, but rather upon his momentary relationship to the Spirit.

Imagine that the spiritual man is like an AM-FM radio also. At conversion, the believing sinner does not get rid of his old sinful nature (AM); he simply receives a new FM system. The Christian now faces a choice. Will he choose to turn on the AM dial, or will he turn on the FM dial? The spiritual man will turn on the FM dial. Tuning out the world and its attractions, he is now in a position to hear heavenly music and the voice of God edifying his soul through the Scriptures.

The third type of person is the carnal man. He is a "fleshly" person (*sarkinos*, Greek). He is saved (addressed as "brethren" in 3:1). He has the indwelling presence of the Holy Spirit, but he is dominated by the sinful desires of his inner self. His behavior is similar to that of the ordinary, unsaved man: "For ye are yet carnal: for whereas there is among you envying, and strife, and divisions, are ye not carnal, and walk as men?" (3:3). The carnal Christian is capable of doing the very same things as the unsaved man does because he is not walking in the Spirit. Paul wrote,

> This I say then, Walk in the Spirit, and ye shall not fulfil the lust of the flesh. For the flesh lusteth against the Spirit, and the Spirit against the flesh: and these are contrary the one to the other: so that ye cannot do the things that ye would (Gal 5:16-17).

In the struggle between the flesh and the Holy Spirit for the domination of the believer's will, the carnal Christian yields to the flesh. Because he is not yielded to the Holy Spirit, he is not in a position to receive the spiritual nourishment of the Word of God which he needs:

> And I, brethren, could not speak unto you as unto spiritual, but as unto carnal, even as unto babes in Christ. I have fed you with milk, and not with meat: for hitherto ye were not able to bear it, neither yet now are ye able (1 Co 3:1-2).

His need is confession of sin and repentance. He must say no to the flesh and yes to the Spirit.

Imagine that this person is also an AM-FM radio with both units in normal working order. The carnal believer, contrary to the exhortations of Scripture, turns on the AM dial, thus exposing himself to the influence of the world (WBS). To an unsaved person or to an untaught, critical Christian, he will look like an unsaved person and may even be called such.

A Christian also sustains a relationship to spiritual growth. Growth involves time and experience. Maturity is not achieved overnight, either in the physical or spiritual realm. Getting saved is like being born; the believer must then grow and develop.

Peter exhorted his Christian readers, "As newborn babes, desire the sincere milk of the word, that ye may grow thereby: If so be ye have tasted that the Lord is gracious" (1 Pe 2:2-3). A believer should have the same appetite for the Word of God as babies have for the bottle. Did you ever notice how babies shake and quiver and how their lips pucker up at the sight of their nursing bottles? They have tasted the milk before; they like it, and their tiny tummies crave for more. The maturing process within the Christian life never ends. Both young and old Christians can continue to grow.

Some Christians develop quickly; others mature slowly. Two Christians, saved the same number of years, can demonstrate different degrees of maturity. For over ten years, I have observed incoming college freshmen. Some of the eighteen-year-old students act like they are twenty-five, while others think and act as though they were fifteen. Some of them had to grow up fast because their parents died and they had to work hard just to gain admission into college. Some have come from nonchristian families where they had to stand for their faith. Still others have lived sheltered lives wherein they never had to make difficult moral decisions. Rate of growth is tied directly to one's background and experience.

The finest description of the contrast between biblical maturity and immaturity is found in the book of Hebrews:

> Of [Melchizedek] we have many things to say, and hard to be uttered, seeing ye are dull of hearing. For when for the time ye ought to be teachers, ye have need that one teach you again which be the first principles of the oracles of God; and are become such as have need of milk, and not of strong meat. For every one that useth milk is unskilful in the word of righteousness: for he is a babe. But strong meat belongeth to them that are of full age, even those who by reason of use have their senses exercised to discern both good and evil (Heb 5:11-14).

What then are the biblical principles underlying spiritual maturity? A *mature* believer should be able to teach others, both from his knowledge of Scripture and from his years of Christian living. As a spiritual adult, he can prepare his own meals from the Scriptures; he does not have to be nursed or spoon-fed. His spiritual senses have been sharpened to make correct moral decisions. His spiritual body (mind and muscles) is well conditioned and coordinated.

The *immature* Christian is just the opposite. Bible teachers have a hard time trying to make spiritual truth simple enough for him to understand. He is dull of hearing, apathetic, indifferent at times to the preached Word. He has been saved long enough to be a spiritual college graduate, but actually he is still in first grade, learning his spiritual ABCs. He is ignorant of basic biblical principles, therefore he cannot relate the Scriptures to his daily practical problems. He has to be told what is right or wrong; he cannot make that distinction by himself. He is entirely dependent upon others; he has no spiritual stability of his own. The need of the immature man is growth.

Maturity involves time. Christians can be found at each

level of the maturing process. Each day should move one
that much closer to conformity to Jesus Christ *if* he learns,
works, and makes decisions under the influence of the
Holy Spirit. Too often, however, some have been saved for
twenty years but have the spiritual aptitude of a five-year-
old. Those wasted years cannot be regained, but the person can begin to grow if he applies himself. In the natural
realm, suppose you have a perfect ten-year-old boy. His
development may be ideal up to this point, but there is
still room for new growth. So it is with a Christian. He
may have growth for ten years (a perfect ten-year-old),
but there is still room for improvement.

Christians are often criticized needlessly and wrongfully. Many of the critics are totally unaware of the different types of believers there can be. First, a Christian
could be both immature and carnal. This means that he
has been saved just a short while and that he is not yielded
to the indwelling Holy Spirit. Second, a Christian could be
mature but carnal. Yes, a spiritual leader, like an evan-
gelist, pastor, Bible professor, or head deacon, could know
the Word and have walked with the Lord for a long time,
and yet for a given moment be yielded to self rather than
to the Spirit. Dr. John Walvoord, the president of Dallas
Theological Seminary, once remarked to a class, "The
closer you get to the spiritual giants, the more you realize
that they too have feet of clay."

Third, a person could be immature but spiritual. This
believer could be totally yielded to God and yet make mistakes because of his inexperience. Fourth, the ideal believer is both mature and spiritual. He has developed from
spiritual infancy to adulthood and is also yielded to the
indwelling Christ. Fifth, the genuine backslider is probably one who was both spiritual and mature at one time,
but who has retreated to a stagnant life full of carnality.

Although the term *backslider* is never used in the New Testament as a description for the believer, it was used by God for idolatrous Israel: "Turn, O backsliding children, saith the LORD; for I am married unto you" (Jer 3:14). The backsliding Israelite was still regarded as a covenant believer, and the basis of return was the fact that God was still married to her. Sin did not bring a loss of salvation or covenant position, only a temporary separation and a severance of daily blessing.

Many Christians have salvation, but they do not enjoy it. Why? Because they are not sure that they are saved. If they do not *feel* saved, they question their salvation. If they are not perfect in their Christian walk, they are apprehensive about their security. Salvation, however, is not based upon our feelings, but upon faith in what God has said through His Word. God wants us to have salvation, and He wants us to know that we have it. John concluded one epistle with, "These things have I written unto you that believe on the name of the Son of God; that ye may know that ye have eternal life, and that ye may believe on the name of the Son of God" (1 Jn 5:13). Read the first epistle of John now and consider these twelve tests of assurance.

First, have you enjoyed spiritual fellowship with God, with Christ, and with fellow believers? John wrote, "That which we have seen and heard declare we unto you, that ye also may have fellowship with us: and truly our fellowship is with the Father, and with his Son Jesus Christ. And these things write we unto you, that your joy may be full" (1 Jn 1:3-4). Do you enjoy singing the praises of God? Do you enjoy praying to Him, thanking Him for all that He has done for you, and asking Him for His direction? Is your heart warmed by the preaching of the Word and by the exaltation of Christ? If you can answer yes to these questions, you are displaying one quality of a Christian.

Second, do you have a sensitivity to sin? John wrote:

> This then is the message which we have heard of him, and declare unto you, that God is light, and in him is no darkness at all. If we say that we have fellowship with him, and walk in darkness, we lie, and do not the truth: But if we walk in the light, as he is in the light, we have fellowship one with another, and the blood of Jesus Christ his Son cleanseth us from all sin. If we say that we have no sin, we deceive ourselves, and the truth is not in us. If we confess our sins, he is faithful and just to forgive us our sins, and to cleanse us from all unrighteousness. If we say that we have not sinned, we make him a liar, and his word is not in us (1 Jn 1:5-10).

Are you aware of the fact that God is absolutely holy? When you deliberately sin, do you sense that your fellowship with your heavenly Father has been broken? Have you confessed your sins and enjoyed the spiritual refreshment that comes with divine forgiveness and cleansing? What many Christians fail to realize is the fact that even when they are enjoying fellowship with God, there is an unconscious cleansing process taking place in their lives. We have impurities and flaws of which we are totally aware. Just being close to God erases some of them.

Third, are you basically obedient to the commandments of Scripture? John wrote:

> And hereby we do know that we know him, if we keep his commandments. He that saith, I know him, and keepeth not his commandments, is a liar, and the truth is not in him. But whoso keepeth his word, in him verily is the love of God perfected: hereby know we that we are in him (1 Jn 2:3-5).

Present keeping of God's commandments is an indication that we were saved (a completed act) and are saved (present standing before God). To what extent must one keep God's commandments? Must he keep all of them all of the time in order to have assurance? God said to Solomon, "And if thou wilt walk in my ways, to keep my statutes and my commandments, as thy father David did walk, then I will lengthen thy days" (1 Ki 3:14). Did David keep all of the divine commandments all of the time? Certainly not. In his sin with Bathsheba, he violated several of them. But as God viewed David's entire life, David was a commandment keeper.

Fourth, what is your attitude toward the world and its values? John admonished, "Love not the world, neither the things that are in the world. If any man love the world, the love of the Father is not in him? (1 Jn 2:15). It is possible for a Christian at times to love the desires and attractions of the world. It is misplaced love; it is wasted love; but he can do it, if he yields to the lust of the sin nature. Demas forsook Paul in Rome because he loved this present world (2 Ti 4:10). However, if a man's entire life is world-centered, then he is not saved. If he daily walks according to the course of this world, then he is still a member of the world system, and he is lost (cf. Eph 2:2).

Fifth, do you love Jesus Christ and look forward to His coming? Paul said that a crown of righteousness would be given to those that love His appearing (2 Ti 4:8). Do you look upward toward heaven because you have looked backward toward Calvary? John wrote,

> Beloved, now are we the sons of God, and it doth not yet appear what we shall be: but we know that, when he shall appear, we shall be like him; for we shall see him as he is. And every man that hath this hope in him purifieth himself, even as he is pure (1 Jn 3:2-3).

Has the fact that Christ could come at any moment changed your life? Do you want to be ready when He comes? Are you confident that when He returns He will take you back into heaven?

Sixth, do you practice sin less now that you have professed faith in Christ? John wrote,

> And ye know that he was manifested to take away our sins; and in him is no sin. Whosoever abideth in him sinneth not: whosoever sinneth hath not seen him, neither known him (1 Jn 3:5-6).

Christ did not save a person in order that that person might sin more in his Christian experience. If genuine conversion has occurred, there has to be a change in the life habits of the person. Since a believer is in Christ and He is in the believer, there will automatically be less sin committed. The holy presence of Christ will prevent such expression of the sin nature.

Seventh, do you love other believers? John wrote, "We know that we have passed from death unto life, because we love the brethren. He that loveth not his brother abideth in death" (1 Jn 3:14). Can anything be clearer? Do you love to be with Christians rather than with the world's unsaved? More than that, do you love Christians for who they are and for who indwells them? Is there a closer bond between you and a fellow believer than there is between you and an unsaved relative?

Eighth, have you experienced answered prayer? Have you gone to your heavenly Father in prayer and have you asked Him for something definite? Have you received a plain answer? John wrote: "And whatsoever we ask, we receive of him, because we keep his commandments, and do those things that are pleasing in his sight" (1 Jn 3:22). Later, he added,

> And this is the confidence that we have in him, that, if
> we ask anything according to his will, he heareth us: And
> if we know that he hear us, whatsoever we ask, we know
> that we have the petitions that we desired of him (1 Jn
> 5:14-15).

Answered prayer is based upon obedience to the revealed
will of God in the Scriptures and upon the purpose of the
heart to do things pleasing to God. So, if you have prayed
in simple, childlike faith and God has responded, you are
experiencing one of the blessings of the Christian life.

Ninth, do you have the inner witness of the Holy Spirit?
John wrote, "Hereby know we that we dwell in him, and
he in us, because he hath given us of his Spirit" (1 Jn
4:13; cf. 3:24). The indwelling presence of the Holy Spirit
is the guarantee of our salvation, but how do we know
that He lives within us? Paul wrote, "For as many as are
led by the Spirit of God, they are the sons of God" (Ro
8:14). Have you ever been led by the Spirit? Has He led
you in the selection of a vocation? Of a certain college?
Of your life's companion? Can you look at the circumstances behind your life and know for sure that God has
led in your life? If so, you have discovered another expression of your sonship in Him. Paul also said, "For ye
have not received the spirit of bondage again to fear; but
ye have received the Spirit of adoption, whereby we cry,
Abba, Father" (Ro 8:15).

Tenth, do you have the ability to discern between spiritual truth and error? John wrote,

> Beloved, believe not every spirit, but try the spirits
> whether they are of God: because many false prophets
> are gone out into the world. Hereby know ye the Spirit of
> God: Every spirit that confesseth that Jesus Christ is
> come in the flesh is of God: And every spirit that con-
> fesseth not that Jesus Christ is come in the flesh is not of

God: and this is that spirit of antichrist, whereof ye have
heard that it should come; and even now already is it in
the world. Ye are of God, little children, and have overcome them: because greater is he that is in you, than he
that is in the world. They are of the world: therefore
speak they of the world, and the world heareth them. We
are of God: he that knoweth God heareth us; he that is
not of God heareth not us. Hereby know we the spirit of
truth, and the spirit of error (1 Jn 4:1-6).

Jesus said that His sheep (believers) recognized His voice,
but that they would not follow the voice of a stranger (Jn
10:3-5, 27). A true believer can sense danger and error in
teaching that does not match up with the revealed Word.
It does not "smell," "sound," or "taste" right to him. He has
that sixth sense, the whisper of the Holy Spirit. Error often
is found not in what is said but in what is not said. Absence of truth is just as wrong as the denial of truth. If you
have identified doctrinal error in a magazine that you have
read or in a radio message that you have heard, then this
discernment is a sign that you have spiritual life.

Eleventh, do you believe the basic doctrines of the
faith? John wrote, "Whosoever believeth that Jesus is the
Christ is born of God" (1 Jn 5:1). Do you believe correctly? Do you believe that He is God manifest in human
flesh, made possible through the virgin conception? Do
you believe that He died on the cross for the sins of the
world? For *your* sins? Do you believe that He was resurrected bodily? Do you believe that He is in heaven and
that one day He will come again? Do you believe that
apart from faith in Christ all men are lost? Have you believed in Him and have you received Him as your personal
Saviour? If so, then you are a genuine Christian.

Twelfth, have you experienced persecution for your
Christian position? Paul encouraged the Philippian be-

lievers not to be "terrified by your adversaries: which is to them an evident token of perdition, but to you of salvation, and that of God" (Phil 1:28). Jesus said that the world would hate and persecute Christians because they hated and persecuted Him first (Jn 15:18-20). This animosity has a double significance. It is a sign that the persecutor is lost and a sign that the persecuted one is saved. Have people ridiculed you for carrying a Bible? Have they called you a sissy or deacon? Have you lost friends or job opportunities because you would not participate in unholy activities? Rejoice and be glad! It is a mark of being a Christian.

The tests of genuine salvation have just been given. What has been your response? Are you convinced that Jesus is your Saviour, or do you still lack assurance? John wrote,

> And hereby we know that we are of the truth, and shall assure our hearts before him. For if our heart condemn us, God is greater than our heart, and knoweth all things. Beloved, if our heart condemn us not, then have we confidence toward God (1 Jn 3:19-21).

Jeremiah said that "the heart is deceitful above all things, and desperately wicked: who can know it?" (Jer 17:9). You may be saved, but the feelings of your heart may not give you that inner confidence you need. In that case, do not listen to your feelings. Listen to the voice of God. Have you done what you are supposed to do to gain salvation? Are some of the signs of salvation evident in your life? If so, on the basis of what God has said, you are a saved person.

If, after reading this book, you are convinced that you are not a genuine Christian, then admit your sinful, moral guilt to God. With an open heart, believe that Jesus Christ died on the cross for your sins and that He rose again for your justification. With open arms, receive and embrace Him as your Saviour. Then confess Him before men with your voice and with your life.

May we all thank God for His unspeakable gift of eternal salvation. May we join the heavenly chorus in singing, "Worthy is the Lamb that was slain to receive power, and riches, and wisdom, and strength, and honour, and glory, and blessing" (Rev 5:12).

Scripture Index

OLD TESTAMENT

GENESIS

1:26-27	15
2:17	23, 90
3:7-13	20, 93
5:3	24
8:21	25
9:6	15
17:9-14	51

EXODUS

20	17
32:32-33	156

NUMBERS

23	105-6

DEUTERONOMY

18:15-22	17
29:29	17

JUDGES

13-15	160-61

1 SAMUEL

9-16	161-63

ESTHER

4:11	44

JOB

14:4	27
15:14	27
42:5-6	104

PSALMS

8:4	32
14:1	14
19:1	14
51	164-65
51:5	25, 28
69:28	156
139:14	14

ECCLESIASTES

7:20	28

ISAIAH

6:5	104
14:12-17	19
55:7-8	99

JEREMIAH

17:9	24

EZEKIEL

3:17-18	129-30
28:12-19	19

AMOS

3:2	36

JONAH

4:2	100

MALACHI

3:14-16	95

NEW TESTAMENT

MATTHEW

3:17	47
4:8-9	21
5-7	26
7:17-20	90
7:21-23	114-15, 167
7:24-27	49
10:32-33	131
11:20-24	17
12:31-32	132-34
12:34	25
12:43-45	134-35
13	143
16:16	49
18:23-25	145
21-22	146-47
22:14	39
24:13	136-37
24:37—25:30	148
25:41	19
27:3-5	166
27:24-25	130

185

MARK

7:20-23	25

LUKE

6:32-35	78
10:20	67
11:13	27
12:48	17
13:25-27	145
15:21-24	99
16:19-31	30
19:10	13, 31
22:31-32	83
24:44	17

JOHN

1:4-5	22, 29
1:12-13	54, 65
3:1-8	54, 88
3:14-16	88
3:18	18, 64
3:36	30
4:13-14	88-89
4:24	16
5:24	64, 71
5:46	17
6:35-51	84, 89-90
6:60-66	115
8:31-32	91
8:42-44	20
9:41	22
10:25-30	50, 75-76, 91
12:31	20
13:8-10	55, 100, 165
14:6	29
14:16-17	86
14:20	47
15:1-6	126-27
15:16	38
15:18-19	19, 38
17	50, 62, 75, 82
17:6	19
17:21	47
18:36	19

ACTS

1:5	56
1:24-25	166-67
2:2	56
2:23	36
8:9-24	167-69
15:18	37
18:9-10	50
20:26-27	130
26:18	58

ROMANS

1:18-23	14-15
2:1, 15	16
2:28-29	51
3:2	17
3:9-20	26, 29, 40
3:22	40
3:24-26	41, 59
3:28	41
4:4-6	107
4:17	46
5:1	64
5:2	43
5:6-10	24, 78-79
5:12-19	22-24, 52
6:3-4	52
6:14	61
6:17-19	25
7:4-10	61
7:12	30
7:14	26
8:1	46, 64, 71
8:3	30
8:9	28, 47, 57
8:14-15, 17	45
8:18	46
8:23	37, 45, 56
8:24-25	31
8:28	39, 46, 79-80
8:29	35, 37
8:30	40
8:33-34	38, 42, 82
8:38-39	72
9-11	110-12
9:6-7	116
9:10-13	38
9:14-21	81
10:8-11	132
10:13	39
11:17-24	128
12:1-2	97
12:5	51
16:17-18	117

1 CORINTHIANS

1:2	62, 105
1:18	18
1:30	40, 62
2:9-10	47
2:9–3:4	171-74
2:12	57
2:14	18
3:9-15	49, 96, 123
5:5	138
6:9-10	60

6:11	41, 55, 60, 62
6:19	47, 57
8:8-12	124
9:26-27	125-26
11:27-32	128-29
11:32	64
12:13	56
15:1-14	18, 121
15:56	61
15:58	95

2 CORINTHIANS

1:22	56-57
3:7	61
4:3	13
4:4	21
4:6	22
5:14-15	66, 97
5:17	65
5:18-20	42
5:21	40
11:13-15	116-17

GALATIANS

1:7-9	108
2:20	53
2:21	107
3:3	109
3:13	61
3:21	30
3:22	26
3:23-25	61
3:26—4:7	65
4:5	45, 61
4:6	57
4:7	45, 69
4:19-31	109
5:2	109
5:1-4	122
6:15	66

EPHESIANS

1:3	34
1:4	38
1:5-6	37, 45, 47, 80
1:7	59
1:11	73
1:14	56, 57
1:18	45
1:22-23	52
2:1	62
2:2	19, 21
2:7	34, 80
2:8-10	77
2:11	51
2:12	28-30, 43

2:13	43
2:16-19	43-44
2:20-22	68
4:1	40, 98
4:6	47
4:17-18	22, 24
4:30	57
4:32	60
5:8	69
5:25-27	63, 87
5:28-30	52
6:12	21, 58

PHILIPPIANS

2:12-13	81
3:3	51
3:9	40, 48
3:10-14	101-2, 142
3:20	67

COLOSSIANS

1:12	63
1:13	20, 48, 57
1:22-23	94
2:9-10	53
2:11	51
2:12	52
2:13	59
3:3-4	46
3:12-17	39

1 THESSALONIANS

1:1	46
1:3	31
1:3-7	39
2:12	48
4:13	31
5:23-24	74
5:24	40, 48

1 TIMOTHY

1:13-15	59, 104
1:19-20	138
2:3-6	39
4:1-3	120

2 TIMOTHY

1:9	108
1:12	74
2:19	57
3:16	16-17
4:18	74

TITUS

1:1	39
2:11-14	67, 91
3:5	55

HEBREWS

1:1-2	14
2:2-3	150
3:12-14	150
5:9	85
5:11-14	175
6:4-6	152-53
6:10	95
6:16-19	72
7:9-10	23
7:25	82
9:15	69
9:24-28	83
10:14	63
10:19-22	44
10:26-27	153
11:13-16	68
12:6-8	135
12:14	27
12:22-23	67
13:5	72

JAMES

2:14-26	41, 92
4:4	19
4:8	43
5:19-20	140

1 PETER

1:2	36, 38
1:4	69
1:5	73
1:16	62
1:19	58
1:20	36
1:23	54
2:4	39
2:5-9	48, 66
2:9	67
3:18	85

2 PETER

1:10	93
1:11	48

1:20-21	17
2	118-119
2:6-9	158
3:9	39

1 JOHN

1	98, 177-78
1:9	55, 60
2:1	83, 103
2:2	59
2:3-5	178-79
2:19	117
3:2-3	37, 63, 179
3:6-10	20, 100-101
3:23	57
4:1-6	181-82
4:17	41, 105
5:1	182
5:12	29
5:13	177
5:16-17	141
5:19	21

2 JOHN

9	93

JUDE

1	74
3-4	120
19	28
24	73

REVELATION

1:17	104
2:5	127
3:5	157
20:10	19
20:11-15	30
22:18-19	154